Supervising Technical and Professional People

Wiley Series in Training and Development

Editor:
Charles T. Peers, Jr.

Succession Planning: Key to Corporate Excellence
by Arthur X. Deegan, II

Supervising Technical and Professional People
by Martin M. Broadwell and Ruth Sizemore House

Supervising Today: A Guide for Positive Leadership, 2nd Edition
by Martin M. Broadwell

Moving Up to Supervision, 2nd Edition
by Martin M. Broadwell

Supervising Technical and Professional People

Martin M. Broadwell
and
Ruth Sizemore House

A Wiley-Interscience Publication

JOHN WILEY & SONS
New York / Chichester / Brisbane / Toronto / Singapore

Publication Data:

nd professional people.

training and development)
terscience publication."
graphy: p.
Includes index.
1. Supervision of employees. 2. Personnel management. I. House, Ruth. II. Title. III. Series.
HF5549.B8565 1986 658.3′044 85-26628
ISBN 0-471-81785-6

Printed in the United States of America

10 9 8 7 6 5 4 3 2

To Martin, Jr., who—being in the real world—
keeps me honest in technical supervision.

Martin M. Broadwell, Sr.

For my favorite bibliophile—Margaret Sizemore Douglass.

Ruth Sizemore House

Preface

Why a book on supervising technical and professional people? Are they so different they have to be written about separately? Do they have to be separated from the masses to avoid contamination of all concerned? Is there a possibility that technical and professional people are simply human beings who act and react like normal people?

These are questions we've been asked before and questions we even asked ourselves. With the years of experience we've amassed in supervising and training both technical and nontechnical employees, we think we know a lot of the answers. Basically, we believe there is enough uniqueness in the technical job as well as the typical technical person to warrant a book for those who supervise them.

This is in no way an indictment of the high-tech environment or population. It is not wrong to be different (any more than it is different to be wrong). If we can deal with some areas where there are identifiable differences, we can make this job easier for supervisors.

What about the many areas where there is little or no difference between technical and nontechnical people? We've tried to deal equally well with those.

What's so special about this book? It's a special response to the many technical managers who have shared their concerns with us. We've tried to make it fit their needs by avoiding a "canned" management principles approach and by doing the following:

Showing how problems—often dealt with only theoretically—look in real life in a technical organization.

Showing some practical real-life solutions for problems. For emphasis, these step-by-step approaches are shown in boxes throughout the book: in our discussions, in chapter summaries, and in an appendix at the end of the book.

Using conversational, "real-world" language.

Combining successful experience (for practical application) and credible research (for a solid decision base).

Facing the issue that supervisors must deal with both the skills and the emotions of their people. (Although people aren't always logical, it's possible to use logic in handling them.)

Real life in a technical organization. To put problems and solutions in a real-life setting, we've built an organization—Broadhouse, Inc.—around the typical functions of a technical organization. Broadhouse, Inc., is a manufacturing company that requires both a research and development division and an engineering division to remain competitive. Most of our case studies and examples are built around these two support functions.

So throughout the book, you'll be meeting these key people, among others:

JIM SWALES, vice president of operations

KENNETH BEYERS, vice president of science and engineering

MATT STEPHENS, manager of research and development, and his staff

BILL MORRIS, manager of engineering, and his staff

The following chart shows where these people are located in the organization.

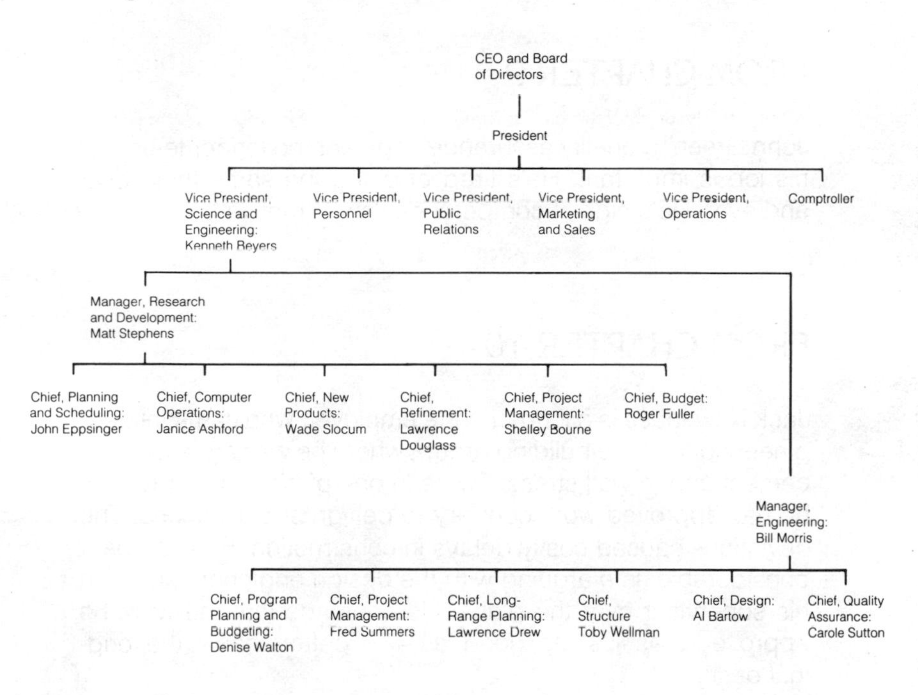

Real-life solutions for problems. Sometimes a solution has high payoffs. Sometimes it only produces the "least worst" result. Each one is "real world" in context. We suggest concrete, step-by-step solutions for problems such as the following:

FROM CHAPTER 1

Wade Slocum is brilliant and abrasive. He leaves behind him a trail of frayed nerves, anger, and—sometimes—deep resentment. Matt Stephens, Wade's supervisor, is constantly weighing the value of Wade's technical ability to the organization. Matt spends a lot of time and energy insulating his group from Wade's apparently random aggression. At what point is his technical value outweighed by human cost?

FROM CHAPTER 9

John Green, a quality assurance engineer, no longer feels that his job is important. He's tired of doing the same thing over and over. He's high in competence, low in motivation.

FROM CHAPTER 10

Jack Newhouse is a long-service employee who came into engineering from the building group, where he was an "expert" in cement and in wall stress. Twice in one of his recent projects he has approved work contrary to design specifications. The deviations caused costly delays in construction. He has spent considerable time arguing with the design engineers and with his supervisor over the plans. He contends that the work he approved was just as good as—or better than—the original design.

FROM CHAPTER 14

Janice Ashford was selected for a significant promotion. Several other employees in the research and development group had hoped to get the job. They experienced Janice's good fortune as a significant loss in their careers.

What's so special about this book? Read on.

MARTIN M. BROADWELL
RUTH SIZEMORE HOUSE

Decatur, Georgia
Kennesaw, Georgia
April 1986

Contents

Supervising Technical and Professional People

chapter one

What's So Special about Supervising Technical and Professional People?

INTRODUCTION

> Programmers have pretty well been the masters of their own destinies throughout the decade. They have been well paid; they have named their hours of work; they have hopped from job to job with impunity, leaving behind desk fulls of chaos; they have been wined and dined, coddled and humored, promoted and pampered. If ever a group of employees rose to Cinderelladom overnight, the computer specialists were that group. They were immune to control; they were immune to discipline; they were immune to competition. (Synders & Lasden, 1980, p. 47)

The computer manager we've quoted here isn't alone. Many experienced managers share his discouragement about supervising technical or professional people. And many new managers approach their jobs with anxiety because of the widespread reputation technical and professional people have for being "unmanageable."

It's true that technical and professional people as a group share some characteristics that can make supervising them a special challenge. Management researchers tell us that responsibility for the work of others is one of the most reliable predictors of conflicting expectations in an organization. Furthermore, they add, responsibility for the work of technical people multiplies the conflict. Technical managers—perhaps more than others—are caught in the middle between the administrative demands of top management and the technical precision and freedom demanded by those they supervise.

In this chapter we take a closer look at the distinguishing characteristics of technical and professional people and discuss ways that managers can capitalize on these characteristics in their management styles.

As a group, technical and professional people are likely to:

Be highly specialized

Be awkward or abrasive in relationships with nontechnical people (perhaps the degree of specialization comes into play here)

Have a relatively high need for professional growth coupled with a relatively low need for social interaction

Be less "in awe" of top management than are other employees

Be more loyal to their technology or profession than to their organization

Enjoy taking calculated technical risks

Expect a pleasant work environment

Expect—perhaps even demand—respect for their personal values

Need help in managing the flow of information

General Guidelines

To respond to the characteristics of technical and professional people, technical managers can:

1. Keep the big picture in focus for their employees
2. Let their own behavior be an example of good interpersonal relations.
3. Groom the people they supervise for professional growth and advancement.

How do these characteristics show up at work? How can a manager respond to them in his or her supervisory style? To see, let's look at Matt Stephens, research and development division manager of an international firm. Matt's style in managing three of his employees illustrates some guidelines for good technical management. These guidelines are appropriate in managing any group of people, but the need for following them is especially important in thc management of technical and professional people.

MANAGING TECHNICAL AND PROFESSIONAL PEOPLE

Keep the Big Picture in Focus

First Janice Ashford, computer section chief. Janice is 28 years old. She's bright and quick and seems impatient with those who aren't. Actually, she just doesn't feel that comfortable around people, period. Her discomfort sometimes comes across as aloofness. Janice clearly wants to be the best and to be recognized for it. But she's so ill at ease around people that it may be hard for her to handle the visibility and the interaction that comes with recognition. Janice doesn't participate in "covered dish" get-togethers that some of the division staff organize. And she doesn't often even socialize with the staff of her own section. In fact, she seems to guard her privacy jealously. She dodges any questions or discussions about her private life—even seems a little annoyed that it ever comes up. Whenever the subject of a conversation shifts from computers or software, Janice seems lost.

When there is a crisis atmosphere at work, the corner of Janice's desk is stockpiled with junk food from the snack food machine. Physically, she's petite; people wonder how she can put away so much food.

Because Janice is so highly focused on her own specialty, Matt regularly reminds her of the big picture. It's hard for Janice to keep the concerns of top management—or even the concerns of her clients in research and development—in mind because she is investing herself with such concentration on technical excellence. (Of course, her commitment to technical excellence is one of the traits that makes her so valuable to the organization.)

For example, on a recent project that had attracted the attention of top management, Janice was reluctant to release a program because she felt that "with a little more time, it could be perfect." Since he was prepared for her reluctance, Matt related the time frame to the operating needs of the company whenever he and Janice discussed the schedule.

> "When Wade gets this new program, he'll be able to show marketing exactly how our customers can use Sentry-12."
>
> "Wade will need the program by May 30 to build it into his presentation to marketing. Let me know of any problems you see with that deadline in time to authorize some overtime if necessary."

> "With your program to back him up, Wade believes he can get the marketing folks to launch their efforts at the upcoming convention of mechanical engineers."

In one project for Matt's budget specialist, Janice wanted to design a program that went well beyond the capability and the interest of the people who would be using it. Again, Janice defined her goal as state-of-the-art perfection, not service to a particular client for a particular purpose. Again, Matt related the refinement of the product to the purpose it would serve in the organization.

> "If the program were put to a different use, additional capabilities would pay off. But for this purpose and for these users, we can't afford to invest time and staff in refinements that would never be used."
>
> "Let me know when the program satisfies Roger's minimum requirements. Then we'll meet with him and his staff to decide if additional 'nice-to-haves' justify further refinement."

Let Their Own Behavior Be an Example

Perhaps it's Janice's focus on her technical specialty that gives other people the impression that she doesn't even see them. She comes across as being impatient with those who aren't as bright or as quick as she is. Actually, she may just be preoccupied. Whatever the reason, she seems distant to other people. The section secretary seems the most upset by it. Doris feels that she simply cannot please Janice. Janice hasn't made negative comments on Doris's work, but Doris feels that Janice "just seems irritated with me all the time." And Doris takes Janice's lack of participation in social affairs at the office to indicate a "better than thou" attitude.

Matt can help ease the tension between Doris and Janice

some if he remembers that technical groups—even those who work together well—may not show the same kind of "togetherness" that an administrative group might. In a group of generalists, the frequency and extent of social interaction would be a better barometer of how well people worked together to solve a business problem. With a group of technical specialists, the social barometer simply isn't that reliable. The loners who have coffee alone and avoid office parties may collaborate wholeheartedly to solve a technical problem. If Matt sets the pattern by being cordial and relaxed around Janice in spite of her apparent disinterest, others in the office are more likely to follow that pattern themselves. If he remains upbeat and pleasant in the face of her brusqueness, others are more likely to do the same. Janice is more than likely just preoccupied—perhaps unsocial but not antisocial.

Matt's behavior can also give Janice a pattern to follow in her interaction with Doris. If Matt talks to Doris at eye level sitting several feet away rather than towering over her or crowding her desk, Janice is more likely to do the same. If Matt takes the time to clarify technical terms for Doris without talking down to her, Janice is more likely to do the same. If Matt listens to Doris' suggestions and questions and responds supportively, Janice is more likely to do the same.

Groom Employees for Professional Growth and Advancement

Janice is determined to get ahead. Certainly she is capable; but she doesn't seem to recognize that people are as important to her career as capability. When Janice is recognized for her good work, she seems so ill at ease that managers are reluctant to initiate contact. And since Janice doesn't initiate any social contact herself, Matt is concerned that top management will conclude that she just doesn't have

General Guidelines

To respond to characteristics of technical and professional people, technical managers can:

4. Absorb hostility
5. Contain the cost of conflict
6. Allow considerable technical freedom within agreed-upon limits

the interpersonal skill, the social ease, or the "attitude toward people" that it takes to succeed in management positions. In fact, they may be right—for the moment. Matt's strategy to groom Janice for advancement includes several tactics:

He will model the interpersonal skills that he hopes Janice will acquire.

He will see to it that Janice has progressive exposure to higher management. He'll be sure that she has the opportunity to grow more accustomed to the contact and to observe Matt's behavior around other managers.

He will provide training opportunities in interpersonal skills.

He will conscientiously reinforce any attempt that Janice makes at being more "sociable."

He will consistently update Janice on the "big picture" and consistently update management on her progress with key projects.

Absorb Hostility

Next, Wade Slocum, chief of new product development. Wade is a brilliant, impatient man in his early 50s. He came to the company after retiring from the military. He was considered a high-achieving "renegade" in both military and civilian circles. He takes a strong stand on some controversial issues and seems to be unconcerned about the way he's seen by top management. In fact, he almost seems to view management as a necessary evil: he may actually enjoy seeing management's discomfort with his behavior. He is impatient with administrative paperwork and with the people who do it. He leaves behind him a trail of frayed nerves, anger, and—sometimes—deep resentment. More than one excellent secretary has claimed Wade as the "reason for leaving" in an exit interview.

While Janice's interpersonal style seems awkward or abrupt, Wade's style is outright abrasive. It would be easier to shrug off some of his outrageous behavior if he were more predictable. But one day of carefully executed charm seems to get people off guard: they begin to think, "Hmmmh, Wade's turned over a new leaf!" When they have allowed themselves to relax and even to enjoy the new Wade, swoosh—there goes the rug from under them! Enter the old Wade. Some people have been hurt once too often. They just turn to stone around him rather than be tricked or humiliated again. Others openly make derogatory remarks. (Wade seems to enjoy these.) Some actually tremble visibly when he's around.

Matt spends a lot of time and energy insulating his group from Wade's apparently random aggression. He absorbs a lot of hostility simply by listening to people express anger and hurt over their treatment by Wade.

Matt also listens to Wade vent his anger and dissatisfaction. He doesn't express agreement, he doesn't condemn Wade, he just listens. Until he decides how to contain or to cut his losses in dealing with Wade (more on that in Chapter Five), Matt will continue to absorb aggression to keep his group from exploding.

Contain the Cost of Conflict

How can Matt constantly absorb so much aggression without exploding, himself? The focus of conflict will vary from situation to situation, but the state of conflict is sustained. Matt is constantly weighing the value of Wade's technical ability to the organization against the cost of Wade's abrasiveness to the organization. Some up-and-coming competitors would be willing to suffer in order to have Wade's experience and ability on their side. His defection could really cost. On the other hand, his presence is really costing, too. Unless Matt takes precautions, both Matt and his staff will become casualties of the conflict. At what point is technical value outweighed by human cost?

We'll have more to say in Chapter Five. Meanwhile, here are the highlights of Matt's strategy to act as a buffer without becoming a casualty himself. To contain the cost of the conflict to the rest of his staff, Matt will:

Keep enough emotional distance so as not to be drawn into The New Wade/Old Wade Routine. Wade's *behavior* may change drastically from one day to the next, but his *personality* isn't likely to. Matt has learned to expect the unexpected, not to count on The New Wade to stick around for very long.

Recognize that what he, Matt, can observe (and is responsible for managing) is Wade's *behavior,* not his *motives* or *attitudes.* Wade may seem motivated to do harm, but only Wade himself knows. (In fact, Wade himself may not know what makes him "tick.") So when Matt gives feedback or sets limits, he will consistently refer to Wade's behavior —not to his motives. Matt will aim his thinking at Wade's behavior, too. He won't invest much energy in answering the unanswerable question "Why?" (This doesn't mean that he'll cut off an effort by Wade to explain, however.)

Have a clear mental picture of how Wade would act if his behavior were "ideal" from Matt's point of view. (Often people invest too much energy itemizing all the things that are wrong without ever developing a clear picture of what would make them happy.)

Plan a systematic course of action to cut his losses when and if he decides the human cost of employing Wade has gone too high. (More on this in Chapter Five.)

Avoid "waving red flags" himself. However extravagant Wade's behavior gets, Matt will resist the temptation to follow Wade's lead. True, it's Matt's job to influence Wade's behavior; but without a doubt, the behavior he can influence the most is his own. He can control his own temper, his own use of abusive language, his own accusations. He can follow that time-honored folk advice: "Don't get in a hissing contest with a snake." (For one thing, that's a contest the snake was born to win. For another thing, once the contest gets under way, it's hard to tell who's the snake and who isn't!)

Present his ideas to Wade assertively, but not aggressively. He will be explicit and firm without being abusive.

Matt will even do some things he would have thought ridiculous five years ago—before his doctor warned him that job stress was making him a good candidate for a heart attack or stroke. At his doctor's insistence, Matt read about the physical affects of chronic stress (more to come in Chapter Five). And now he sees what he called "silly fads" five years ago as survival skills. To contain the *personal* cost of conflict to him, Matt will:

Use deep-breathing exercises and muscle relaxation exercises at intervals during a high-stress day to help reduce physical and emotional wear and tear.

Practice deep-breathing and muscle relaxation exercises at home *regularly*.

Participate regularly in an aerobic exercise such as biking or swimming.

Get ample sleep.

Eat nutritiously and moderately. (Both nutritional shortages and extra weight can drain energy needed to handle stress.)

Give himself verbal mental encouragement. (That's right, talk to himself! Tell himself things like "This won't be fatal, just unpleasant" or "Yes, I *can* control my temper and still be firm.")

Allow Technical Freedom within Agreed-Upon Limits

Waist deep in alligators, Matt still does a good job of remembering that he's there to drain the swamp: he has not only conflict—but also work flow—to manage. Wade's work quality is usually high. But he does like to take calculated risks. When Matt can establish well-defined parameters, he allows Wade a great deal of technical freedom within those bounds. The end product is rarely disappointing, and it is often spectacular. (Wade's technical risk taking has a better track record than his interpersonal risk taking.)

But Wade's inclined to hold off on completion to allow "a little more time" for experimentation. So (as with Janice) the variable that Matt really needs to manage most closely is time.

General Guidelines

To respond to the characteristics of technical and professional people, technical managers can:

7. Demonstrate respect for personal values
8. Manage the flow of information between their groups and the rest of the organization
9. Manage the flow of information within their groups

Although Wade works for long periods with very loose supervision, Matt establishes checkpoints to spot any schedule slippage early; and he invariably touches base with Wade at the appointed time. When a project does slip behind, Matt works with Wade on the spot to pinpoint the effects on the entire project and to identify right away how they can accommodate the change with the least damage.

Demonstrate Respect for Personal Values

Finally, Roger Fuller, senior budget specialist. Roger is 45 years old. He is competent and generally fairly sociable. He seems out of sorts whenever there's a maintenance problem at the office, though. If there's a problem with the heating or air conditioning, he can be expected to complain continuously until it's repaired. Roger is open in expressing dissatisfaction with something that bothers him. But he can stay rattled for days if a disagreement gets loud or abusive. He expects a lot of "social ease" from his secretary: he expects her to be cordial under any imaginable circumstance and likes her to bring in a coffee tray when he has a visitor in the office.

Roger is very dependable and is generally cooperative about putting in extra hours—except on Sunday. He is straightforward about his belief that Sunday is a day for family and church. Several times during an emergency, he's worked long, hard, and cheerfully on Saturday, but insisted that someone else take care of the work on Sunday. He expects the company to respect his personal values and work around them.

Roger seems to rankle a bit when an administrative directive comes down from above. He feels that the company's personnel/administrative people don't really know what the company's all about. He doesn't think people with "no technical background" should be telling him what to do.

Manage the Flow of Information between Their Group and the Rest of the Organization

For Roger, physical and emotional comfort at the office have high priority. When these comforts are interrupted by an air conditioner or a person who is "acting up," Matt's role as an insulator is again important. He listens to Roger's complaints about the physical temperature good-naturedly. And he listens intently to Roger's concerns about the emotional climate. Again, it isn't as important that Matt *agree* with Roger as it is that he *listen* to Roger. Just listen and acknowledge how things look from Roger's point of view.

It's tougher for Matt to work around some of Roger's personal values. Matt respects them, of course. But Roger is so vocal and so adamant about some—such as reserving Sunday for church and family—that Matt sometimes feels put off about approaching Roger even in an emergency. When it's necessary to schedule an activity for Sunday, however, Matt uses some relaxation techniques and then approaches Roger assertively. He makes no attempt to belittle Roger's value system; in fact, he acknowledges the importance of such values to a satisfying life-style. But sometimes a value they share—getting the work done right and on time—temporarily overrides the others: like getting the oxen out of the ditch. So Matt enlists Roger's support. And if attempts to complete the activity on Saturday don't work, Matt works with Roger to decide if someone else can handle what's left to be done or if Roger must come in.

Of course, a sharp manager doesn't have his oxen in the ditch every Sunday. So handling the technical aspects of management—such as scheduling—well is necessary to give Matt the freedom and the time to attend to the human side of management. Matt cannot afford either the luxury of being lax in technical matters or the luxury of being lax in interpersonal ones. And he must constantly combat a feeling of being overwhelmed by both.

Roger's dislike for administrative directives from above is pervasive. He has trouble sitting through the administrative "rules-setting" phase that is necessary in every project. As far as he's concerned the issues are already black or white: either you can afford to do something or you can't. He's actually a stickler for the rules—or rather *his* rules—but he feels that management is too slow and too dull to avoid unnecessary delays by giving timely authorizations. He'd much prefer to have impenetrable boundaries within which he could work without reporting to or receiving questions from top management.

With Roger and many other technical people the flow of information is critical to performance. Yet the role of a "gatekeeper" to manage the flow of information is one that is often missing altogether in a technical group. Certainly Roger will not spontaneously assume that function. Neither will explosive Wade nor standoffish Janice. Who's left? Right. Matt.

And Matt's job won't be easy. *As information moves across technologies,* it will be subject to a different interpretation in each one. For one thing, different technical languages "translate" the information differently. And specialists in each technology are likely to have a special view of the world that affects the way information is received. To the mechanical engineer, for example, the energy efficiency of a new product may be the only important part of the information. The accountant, on the other hand, may not even notice the energy efficiency; he may see only the dollar cost.

And as information moves up or down the decision hierarchy, different views of the organization are likely to alter it's appearance. Top management, for example, must be concerned about survival issues: How would pending labor laws affect the cost of operating? What can be done to appease conservationists who have won an injunction against plant enlargement? How can the company protect it's market from a competitor with a less expensive product? Closer to an individual client, a service engineer quite appropriately focuses on other issues: How can he decrease turn-around time on reworked equipment? How can he decrease the per item cost of service? What is the most efficient schedule for routine maintenance?

Now all of these issues are perfectly legitimate. But what happens when the service engineer hears on the news about the sizeable company contribution to a community restoration project right after he—the service engineer—has been refused funding for new equipment that would make his work easier and more efficient? Right again. Matt or one of his comanagers is caught in the middle.

Matt has been caught in the middle by surprise more than once. But he's learned several ways to reduce the number of surprises and to reduce the potential damage to morale. He's found his role as gatekeeper between his group and the rest of the organization is less hazardous when he:

Expects communication breakdown whenever he's passing information across two or more boundaries in the organization—either horizontal boundaries (decision-making levels) or vertical boundaries (technical or administrative divisions)

Continuously asks himself this question about everyone in the chain of communication: *Who* expects *what* from *whom* and *when*?

Checks out perceived differences in expectations right away and clarifies or renegotiates them as soon as he can do so without causing *unnecessary* panic or embarrassment.

Double-checks the completeness of information he passes on by asking himself these three questions: (1) What do I want my listener (or reader) to do, to think, or to feel differently as as a result of getting this information? (2) What specific information will my listener need in order to do what I want? (A message without this information isn't complete.) (3) What would help my listener better understand or accept what I want? (A message without this information may be wasted.)

Presents information assertively whenever it is emotionally loaded or controversial.

Manage the Flow of Information within Their Groups

When a group has a lot of experience with the technology behind a project, gatekeeping information within the group becomes especially important. If a project were strictly research, information from outside the group (including information from professionals in other companies) would be critical. But in most technical service projects, the technical expertise is most likely to be somewhere in Matt's group. It may not all be in the head of one person, and it may not even be in the particular team assigned to the project. (That would be ideal, but the people with the most experience in a particular area may already be assigned to a higher-priority or higher-visibility project.) So Matt's gatekeeping of information within his own group is critical. When Janice has the expertise, Matt will need to see that she shares it despite her social awkwardness. When Wade is the expert, Matt will need to see that he shares the needed information without creating havoc. When Roger has the expertise, Matt will need to get it through Roger's "impenetrable boundary" out to the people who need it.

CONCLUSION

Technical and professional people as a group share characteristics that make supervising them a special challenge.

General Guidelines

To respond to the characteristics of technical and professional people, technical managers can:

1. Keep the big picture in focus for their employees
2. Let their own behavior be an example of good interpersonal relations
3. Groom the people they supervise for professional growth and advancement
4. Absorb hostility
5. Contain the cost of conflict
6. Allow considerable technical freedom within agreed-upon limits
7. Demonstrate respect for personal values
8. Manage the flow of information between their groups and the rest of the organization
9. Manage the flow of information within their groups

Many managers share the widely held view that technical people are "unmanageable." And it's true that technical managers—perhaps more than others—are caught in the middle between the administrative demands of top management and the technical precision and freedom demanded by those they supervise.

Successful technical managers take the characteristics of technical and professional people into account. They do a "balancing act" to respond to technical idiosyncracies and to management requirements at the same time.

chapter two

What Do We Know about People in General?

INTRODUCTION

Despite their distinguishing characteristics, technical people were people before they were technical. They have more characteristics in common with the rest of the human race than characteristics that distinguish them. So technical managers can expect much of what they know about people in general to help them manage technical and professional people in particular. In this chapter we review some things we know about people in general and explore ways that technical managers can make the most of that general knowledge.

How are technical and professional people like people in general? Mostly. Like others, technical and professional people want to feel that they are doing something worthwhile and that they are doing it well. Like other people, they will be most motivated by the prospect of satisfying needs that are going *un*met at a particular time. And those unmet needs will be different for different people. In fact, those unmet needs will be different for the same person at different times. Like others, technical and professional people are likely to stay in their jobs only if certain kinds of needs are met. They are likely to improve their performance, however, only if certain other kinds of needs are met. ("Hard-driving high achievers" from technical or nontechnical groups may not be covered in this generalization: some management studies suggest that their driving need for achievement motivates improved performance whenever improvement is possible—regardless of the external conditions!) And it follows that for managers of technical and professional people, as for managers of people in general, the same guiding principle holds true: Know the people you manage as individuals; manage them as individuals.

Technical and professional people are mostly like people in general? Skeptical? Then see if you find any surprises in the way a group composed largely of technical and professional people responded to a questionnaire about work.

First, complete the following questionnaire yourself. Put a "1" by the job characteristic you think is most important to the technical and professional people you supervise (or will supervise). Put a "2" by the second most important characteristic, a "3" by the third most important characteristic, and so on, until you've put a number by every characteristic.

_____ Friendliness of people in work group
_____ Amount of freedom on the job
_____ Respect received from work group
_____ Way they are treated
_____ Job security
_____ Chances to accomplish something worthwhile
_____ Fringe benefits
_____ Chances to do something that makes them feel good about themselves
_____ The resources they have to do their own jobs
_____ Chances to learn new things

_____ Chances to do the things they do best
_____ Opportunity to develop skills and abilities
_____ Physical surroundings of the job
_____ Chances to take part in making decisions
_____ Amount of praise they get for a job well done
_____ Amount of pay they get
_____ Amount of information they get about their job performance
_____ Chances for getting a promotion

Adapted from Patricia A. Renwick, and Edward E. Lawler, What you really want from your job, 1978, *Psychology Today, 11*(12), pp. 53–58, 60, 62, 65, 118. Adapted by permission from The American Psychological Association.

To see how the original group ranked these items on importance and on satisfaction with them, look at the chart on the following page.

Now take a closer look at the job characteristics ranked as the top five in importance:

1. Chances to do something that makes them feel good about themselves
2. Chances to accomplish something worthwhile
3. Chances to learn new things
4. Opportunity to develop new skills and abilities
5. Amount of freedom on the job

Were you surprised to find some of these items rated so highly? Supervisors are often surprised that these items ranked higher than things like amount of pay (ranked 12), fringe benefits (ranked 16), or job security (ranked 11).

But the value given these job characteristics is what we've been told to expect from the "new worker." For example, Morris Massey (1978) compares values of the "traditional genera-

Importance	Satisfaction	
14	1	Friendliness of people in the work group
5	2	Amount of freedom on the job
8	3	Respect received from the work group
13	4	Way they are treated
11	5	Job security
2	6	Chances to accomplish something worthwhile
16	7	Fringe benefits
1	8	Chances to do something that makes them feel good about themselves
7	9	Resources they have to do their job
3	10	Chances to learn new things
6	11	Chances to do the things they do best
4	12	Opportunity to develop skills and abilities
18	13	Physical surroundings of the job
10	14	Chances to take part in making decisions
15	15	Amount of praise they get for a job well done
12	16	Amount of pay they get
9	17	Amount of information they get about their job performance
17	18	Chances for getting a promotion

Adapted from Patricia A. Renwick and Edward E. Lawler, What you really want from your job, 1978, *Psychology Today, 11*(12), pp. 53–58, 60, 62, 65, 118. Adapted by permission from The American Psychological Association.

tion" with the values of the new "rejectionist generation" this way:

Values of the Traditional Generation	Value of the Rejectionist Generation
Group orientation	Individuality
Authority	Participation
Institutional leadership	Questioning
Conformity	Self-expression
Materialism	Experience
Money	"Having a nice day"

Classical management theories can accommodate technical and "rejectionist" values together with more traditional ones. Why mention *theories* at all when dealing with practicing supervisors? The real world is never as cut and dried as the theories would have you believe. True, but the theories worth knowing (well researched and tested through experience over time) can help managers do at least two very practical things. First, they help managers decide when it's time to put previous assumptions aside—when it's time to explore a situation one on one with an employee. Second, the theories can help managers organize—and do something with—the information that results from that joint exploration.

EMPLOYEES AS INDIVIDUALS

One classical management theory that we feel is worth knowing is Maslow's hierarchy of needs. According to Maslow's theory, a person must substantially satisfy needs at all lower levels before the prospect of satisfying higher-level needs will be motivating. Maslow grouped needs into five "levels."

Level One: Physical Needs. Include food, water, shelter, and sex. These needs must be substantially satisfied before a person can be motivated by needs at any other level.

Level Two: Safety and Security Needs. Develop around the drive to be free from deprivation, to have some assurance that freedom from deprivation will last. Until a person feels substantially free from deprivation, he or she cannot be motivated by needs at the next higher level.

Level Three: Social Needs. Include group belongingness, the need to be accepted by others. Until these needs are substantially met, a person cannot be motivated by needs at the next higher level.

Level Four: Ego Needs. Include mastery and competence, confidence, independence, prestige, status, and good reputation. Until these needs are substantially met, a person cannot be motivated by the highest order of needs.

Level Five: Self-Actualization Needs. Include self-fulfillment and realization of potential.

At what level of need are technical people and members of the rejectionist generation likely to operate? Well, let's see what their values suggest.

Job Characteristics Ranked among the Top Five in Importance	Values of the Rejectionist Generation
1. Chances to do something that make them feel good about themselves	"Having a nice day"
2. Chances to accomplish something worthwhile	Participation

3. Chances to learn new things	Experience
4. Opportunity to develop new skills and abilities	
5. Amount of freedom on the job	Individuality Self-expression Questioning

Values from both lists are likely to be held by people who are motivated to satisfy:

Ego needs	Mastery and competence Confidence Independence Prestige Status Good Reputation
Self-actualization	Self-fulfillment Realization of potential

Maslow's theory can help managers identify benchmarks for conditions at work most likely to motivate at the level of their employees' needs. Actually, the expression "the level" is misleading. True, managers can make some good guesses about their employees as a group based on their technical and professional backgrounds. They can also make some good guesses based on what we know about people in general. But these guesses about employees as a group simply give the technical manager a headstart; they can't tell the manager all that he or she needs to know about individual employees. Only the employees themselves can do that. So after the manager has used a theory like Maslow's to identify some

Managing People in General

Like managers of people in general, technical managers should:

1. Know employees as individuals
2. Manage them as individuals

benchmarks, some critical steps remain: the manager must get to know the employees as individuals and must manage them as individuals. Janice, the competent but socially awkward computer specialist, would be terrified of being "the center of attention." But being "the center of attention" is a condition that Wade (the brash, crackerjack engineer) would flourish under!

CHANGES IN BEHAVIOR

Different employees will operate at different levels of need. In fact, a given person will operate at different levels at different times. A shift in level of need can be a signal that something has changed in a particular employee's life. That signal is a manager's cue to observe the employee with particular care to notice any changes for the better that deserve reinforcement, as well as identifying any areas that call for reassurance.

Again, Janice is a good example. She had been a competent computer specialist with the full range of good work habits. She arrived early, had her work done on time, and—although she always seemed a bit awkward—was unfailingly courteous. Then she became section chief. At first Matt was afraid that he'd made a big mistake in promoting her. She be-

Managing People in General

Like managers of people in general, technical managers should:

3. Spot changes for the better that deserve reinforcement
4. Identify concerns that call for exploration or reassurance

gan showing up late for work, missed (or nearly missed) some important deadlines, and seemed to have changed overnight into a rude, overbearing bundle of nerves.

Matt's impulse was to feel anger and disappointment. But when he took the time to talk to Janice and to think about what was happening, Maslow's theory helped him make some good guesses. Independence, competence, and good reputation were obviously important to Janice. She clearly had enjoyed those things as a computer specialist. But in an unfamiliar role at which she had no experience, all three were at risk. It would make sense for her to feel anxious about them. Furthermore, she had left a situation in which she had been accepted by her peers to enter one in which even acceptance was uncertain. Instead of anger, Matt expressed reassurance and encouragement. Now, after a matter of months, Janice is acting more like Janice: still socially awkward, but also punctual, conscientious, and efficient.

THE JOB ENVIRONMENT AND THE JOB ITSELF

Another classical management theory—Herzberg's motivation-hygiene theory—seems to apply equally well to techni-

Managing People in General

Like managers of people in general, technical managers should:

5. Manage the job environment to control turnover

6. Manage the job itself to control performance

cal management and to general management. In a nutshell, Herzberg's theory says that a manager must manage the job environment, to control turnover, and the job itself, to control performance.

To illustrate, let's look again at Roger, the senior budget specialist. Roger is vocal about any detail that dissatisfies him in his work environment: air-conditioning problems, unpleasantness between coworkers, the absence of any social amenities. It's entirely possible that too much "environmental disturbance" would give Roger cause to look for another job. But throughout his complaining, Roger's performance has not suffered. He has continued to be hardworking and high performing.

With good reason, Matt closely monitors Roger's complaints about the job environment. (As we're using the term here, *job environment* includes company policy, type of supervision, general working conditions, interpersonal relationships, salary, status, and security.) Matt wouldn't want to lose one of his best performers over accumulated inconveniences that could be controlled. When the remedy is actually beyond Matt's control, he is sure to let Roger know what influence he can exert and how he will exercise that influence.

But Matt also closely monitors the relationship between

Roger and his job: Roger's interest in his job, and the opportunities for added responsibility, growth, achievement, recognition, and advancement. If Roger's performance falls into a slump, the problem (and the solution!) is likely to be found in Roger's relationship with the job itself—not in the work environment.

CONCLUSION

Technical people and professional people were people before they were technical. Like other people, they want to do a worthwhile job and do it well. Like other people, they will be motivated by the prospect of satisfying unmet needs. Like other people, they are individuals. So much of what we know about people in general can help the managers of technical people.

Managing People in General

Like managers of people in general, technical managers should:

1. Know employees as individuals
2. Manage them as individuals
3. Spot changes for the better that deserve reinforcement
4. Identify concerns that call for exploration or reassurance
5. Manage the job environment to control turnover
6. Manage the job itself to control performance

chapter three

How Can I Help My Group Communicate with Nontechnical People?

INTRODUCTION

Often technical and professional people are asked to share some of the information they have with people who don't have the technical expertise, training, experience, and background to understand all that is said in a report or in conversation. This frequently creates a problem for both technical and the nontechnical people. Let's notice part of a conversation between Rod Samuelson, an information specialist in the public relations department, and Lawrence Drew, a supervisor in the long-range planning group. It has just been announced that the company is undertaking some rather far-reaching steps to develop an entirely new product line, combining various technologies. Rod has sought out someone with some information he can pass on to the public, since a large number of people will be employed and the construction will use expertise from both the present location and Europe. The public relations department desires to capitalize on this and get as much favorable publicity out of it as possible. Since Larry is in charge of long-range planning and has had a great deal to do with bringing this project together, Rod has met with Larry for lunch in the company cafeteria, and we hear them discussing the matter:

Rod: From what I hear you saying, Larry, this is going to be a rather exciting project that should have a lot of impact on a community or the state of art, as you people are prone to say, on the whole field.

Larry: That's very true. You know, our projections are somewhat conservative at this time. We feel that we have done enough research and tested the market and the product well enough to know that there is a demand and that we have the capability of meeting that demand.

Rod: I'm not sure I understand just exactly what the project is. My goal is to work up some news releases and submit an article or two for some of the newspapers. Perhaps we can even do a Sunday supplement with some pictures showing what is happening to some of our local people and what we're doing for the community. Naturally this will have to be nontechnical, and I'll be glad to check with you before I release anything.

Larry: Well, I would certainly hope you will let me know about anything you are turning loose; because even though we don't have any real secrets to reveal, we need to be concerned with the accuracy. There will be a lot of interest in this, and people need to know that we know what we are talking about.

Rod: I don't plan to get too technical, and I doubt that a lot of technical people will be reading the kind of releases that we are turning out.

Larry: Nevertheless, we strive for accuracy, and part of the story on this release is that we have devised a system for putting together very low tolerance activities.

Rod: Meaning what by "low tolerance"?

Larry: It just means that we don't accept high tolerance in the particular manufacturing system we use on anything that we do. In fact, we have been able to reduce the variance from usual standards to such a small tolerance that we are able to venture into this new product line.

Rod: Okay, so what you're saying is that you've got some high-quality stuff here and you're going to take advantage of that by making something else.

Larry: Well, I wouldn't say it exactly that way. When we use the word "quality," we're usually talking about error free, from the human standpoint as well as the mechanical. In this case we're just talking about a specific product, and we use the term "low tolerance" to avoid confusing people with the word "quality," "assurance," or something of that nature.

Rod: Well, okay. I suppose there is a difference; but tell me a little more about the project, remembering that we are not looking for highly technical things and that my own knowledge of the business is limited to the kind of nontechnical public relations reports that we usually put out.

Larry: Well, I guess the simplest way I can put this is that for a long time it seemed possible for us to take advantage of the expertise we have in our spindal operation and combine that with the optical research that had been going on in our European division. We finally got a breakthrough when we were able to combine some of our computer technology in manufacturing by being able to robotize the operation in order to get the tolerance as low as we have it—somewhere around 0.0001 millimeter in variance. We . . .

Rod: I'm sorry, Larry. I think you've lost me there. What's the "robotize" word that you used?

Larry: (Slight disgust in his voice) We have consistently used robots, mechanical devices that do things on the assembly line; and when you do that, you refer to it as "robotizing."

Rod: Okay, I'm sorry, I'd just never heard that word before.

Larry: Okay, let's see what we were saying. We've found a way of combining our computer technology where we had used the robots to get the very excellent tolerance level. We have a very high efficiency turbodrive system in our interfacing unit, and that enables us in the optical extrusion unit to . . .

Rod: I think I'm having some trouble here, Larry. I'm really trying to get this down a little better, but I don't understand some of the words here. I don't know that I need to use the word "turbodrive system" and I suppose "extrusion unit" and "interface" are just technical terms.

Larry: Sure they're technical terms, but this is a technical operation (disgust showing a little more in his voice). It's not like we're just using a hammer and saw and a pair of pliers, you understand!

Rod: Well I'm sorry. I didn't mean to sound so totally ignorant, but I am writing for the public and the public does have some limitations in what they can understand.

Larry: I understand that they have some limitations; but if we're doing to tell them what we're doing, we might as well tell them *right* instead of just some fancy words that don't meant anything.

What we've just heard is a conversation that's duplicated many times a day in most high-tech fields. We understand Larry's disgust because he's talking to someone who's going to report something that's close to him which he understands very well. He will have to put in a lot of time, thought, and effort to write it out in some way that probably nobody will recognize from the technical standpoint. On the other hand, Rod is completely without the skills, experience, or knowledge to comprehend the technical aspects of what's being said. Neither is at fault, since each is operating from his everyday base or frame of reference. This doesn't make the job any easier. It doesn't help Rod understand what's being said, and it doesn't help Larry explain it any better. We must recognize that there is no way that Rod is going to become an instant expert with the complete ability to understand everything that's being said. The real burden is going to lie on Larry, because he has the job of simplifying the information to the point that the general public can understand it.

Is it possible for these two people ever to communicate in a meaningful way? Is it possible for Larry to put his ideas, concepts, and technical ideas into nontechnical words so that they can be understood? Yes, it is possible, but it's not going to be easy. Larry can neither blame Rod for not having the technical expertise to follow what he's saying, nor put all the blame on him if, when this is over, he still misunderstands and something gets written that Larry finds unacceptable. The real burden of communication is going to fall on Larry. He has the information, but the public is not going to get it unless he provides it for them. The company wants to get a lot of mileage out of this, and Larry must understand that they won't get mileage by talking about things so technical that the general reader won't even know where to begin.

IMPROVING COMMUNICATION WITH OTHER DEPARTMENTS

Let's see what Larry will have to do to improve the communications process:

1. Perhaps the biggest problem to be resolved has to do with Larry's attitude. Most problems in communication between people or groups of people stem from an attitude in one or both toward the responsibility for the communication. In this case Larry thinks that Rod, and maybe most of the nontechnical people in the organization, are really not very smart. He hasn't necessarily come to this conclusion by thinking this out; it just seems that every time he tries to communicate with any of these people, he has very poor success; and since he doesn't have many failures when he's talking to his peers, who are technically oriented, he naturally puts the blame on lack of intelligence of the nontechnical people. He needs to understand that the people he's talking to, including Rod, probably have just as much intelligence as he has and that given the background, experience, training, education, and interests, they might well have the same vocabulary that he does. Larry will have to understand that just not speaking his language or understanding his explanations doesn't mean that these people aren't smart. It just means that their interests, activities, and work assignments lie in different directions.

2. Larry has another attitude that is shared by many technical people. He probably doubts that Rod and the public relations department really serve much of a useful purpose as far as the business is concerned. He sees the real profit coming from the technical people, the engineering people, and those who understand the production process, how we got where we are, and what's happening on the production lines. When he talks to the public relations department and finds that practically nothing that he says is understood, he won-

ders why we even have these people around. He finds it hard to accept that these people have anything useful to contribute since they don't know the language, can't talk about the business, and can't understand and explain the technical aspects of what's really happening in the factory, service, and profit-making activities. He probably feels the same way about the accounting department, the customer relations people, the complaint department, and the human resources people who provide supervisor and management training. Too many technical people think the only ones in the organization who are not a drag on it are those technical people who understand the processes that keep the wheels turning and, as they would say, contribute directly to the profit by keeping production going and by keeping the research going in order to meet the competition. Anybody else is perceived as taking away from the profits and contributing nothing to the furtherance of the cause and the goals of the organization.

All of that may be too broad a generalization, but it is not unusual to find people in Larry's position who have that viewpoint. What Larry will have to do is accept the fact that the organization really knows what it's doing when it puts people in these kinds of jobs. In his own way, Rod probably had to meet as many strenuous interview criteria as Larry did when he went to work. He probably also had to have a specific degree, specific experience, and some very good qualifications in order to get the job. Larry probably feels that just anybody could do Rod's job without much trouble. He sees it as a nontechnical job that requires very little in the way of experience or knowledge of the business; he probably thinks that a simple high school education, or just a little more than that, would satisfy the requirements for the job.

When technical people communicate with nontechnical people, they must do so on a level of respect, not disrespect. It needs to be done on a level of understanding that says, "I think I know my job pretty well; I think I do a pretty good job at it. There are some requirements that I have to have in order to do my job well, and I'm sure there are requirements that you must have to do your job. I'll give you the respect that's due your job and I'll expect the same from you." Nontechnical people do not lack intelligence when they lack the vocabulary, experience, or education to converse at the level or with the vocabulary of technical people.

3. Another of Larry's problems, which is shared with many technical and professional people, is expecting perfection from nontechnical people when they describe the technical aspects of the business. When technical people communicate with nontechnical people, it is necessary for them to understand that the bulk of the world is not only nontechnical, but also not really vitally interested in all of the intricacies and technicalities of much that is technical. Because of this, things will have to be expressed in nontechnical terms; and when this happens, there may be no particular word or phrase that gives the exact meaning with 0.00019 accuracy in describing some particular piece of equipment or phase of the business of operation. A good example was the little bit of contention that Larry had with Rod over the use of the word *quality*. To people in manufacturing and production *quality assurance* has specific meanings these days; for the world in general the word *quality* means doing things right or well. But Larry wasn't content to let Rod use that word in its broader or generic sense; he had to be sure that Rod used the correct interpretation of the word *tolerance*. The truth is that the word *tolerance* has a different meaning to the casual or general reader and it certainly would not be thought of in the same terms as the word *quality*.

4. Finally, Larry needs to develop a better vocabulary. It always comes as a shock to a highly technical, highly skilled professional person that he or she has a poor vocabulary, but it is a fact that Larry and many other highly technical people have not done the kind of reading that develops the vocabu-

lary they need to talk to the less technical people. If we're going to be able to talk to people that don't have or understand our vocabulary, it behooves us to find a vocabulary that will allow us to communicate with them rather than insist that they develop our vocabulary. As we have said, the nontechnical people are intelligent, skilled in their own jobs, and knowledgeable about things that they work with; and when it comes time for the engineering and technical people to communicate with them, they will have to use their own intelligence in developing the language capability to communicate. Since we have talked about attitudes, it might be well to mention that we shouldn't tell ourselves we are developing this vocabulary so that we can condescend to talk to these people who are somehow lesser lights. We are doing it because it makes sense and because we hope they will try the same thing in talking to us. We're doing it for the benefit of the organization, because getting everybody to talk in an understanding manner to as many other people as possible is the best thing for the organization.

Attitudes for Successful Communication with Nontechnical People

To communicate successfully with nontechnical people, technical managers should understand that:

1. Nontechnical is not nonintelligent
2. Nontechnical people are equal contributors in organizational success
3. Complete accuracy in word usage is not a requirement for nontechnical understanding
4. Technical people need to develop nontechnical vocabularies

IMPROVING COMMUNICATION WITH SUBORDINATES

So far we have talked about some things Larry must do to communicate with nontechnical people in other departments, but Larry has some other problems, too. Reporting to Lawrence Drew (Larry) is a research assistant and a clerk typist, both of whom are very competent in what they do. It so happens that they are both nontechnical people in nontechnical jobs. Betty White, the research assistant, sounds as though she has a technical job. In truth her job is exactly as it's described—one of doing research in areas where long-range planning is being done. This may mean looking through commercial records, looking in the library for ratings of various companies, looking through and analyzing newspaper reports of new projects, or collecting data from any number of sources in order for Larry to make certain decisions regarding long-range planning efforts. Betty has a degree in library science and she is good at her job. She has a very organized mind and can stick with a project as long as it takes to get the necessary information. Her brief experience as a librarian helped her understand how information is stored and filed—not just in libraries but in other sources as well. All this makes her a valuable employee. Larry appreciates her and the job that she does; however, there are some obvious problems that can arise if he cannot recognize that she is, in fact, a nontechnical employee.

One of his problems is giving her long, technical explanations, expecting her to carry out his instructions, which he has failed to simplify in more general terms. In this case Larry is lucky because she is information based and is likely to come back to him if she doesn't understand what he wants done; but actually, she is doing what he should be doing. He should be the one to find out if she understands before he leaves the assignment with her. Certainly it would be wrong for him to expect her always to understand everything or to be held accountable if she didn't understand some of the things that were said. Part of Larry's problem is that as he sees her compiling data and organizing it as she is able to do, he may interpret this as a more technical job than it really is. He may lapse into talking to her in technical terms, giving directions to her in ways that he might use to speak to another engineer or technical person. It is important for him to keep in mind that she is skilled, talented, and very competent in what she does, but that her studies have not been along the line of technical and professional education. By the same token he should be careful not to mark her down or fault her during an evaluation for her failure to follow directions or to understand certain things that he says. He must make sure that any criticism that he makes of her is based on her having gotten her instructions in concise, nontechnical terms.

The clerk who works for Larry has an altogether different story. All day Nancy will be typing technical terms. She files under technical terms, spells technical terms, takes dictation of technical terms, and copies things of a technical nature. She's not a technical person and is not trained in the technical aspects of the job. She's not trained in or expected to understand the technical jargon she's typing and sorting. Here again is an opportunity for Larry to misunderstand. Because she is working in a technical section, typing technical things, writing to technical people, and processing technical mail and other documents, she may appear to be understanding a lot of the technical words that confront her. If Larry misinterprets this, he may also give her instructions that she will not understand. He may leave her with misunderstandings or misconceptions about what she's supposed to be doing. Since she has not had the more rigid training of a librarian and is not used to searching for right answers, she may not always draw the right conclusions about the things that she wonders. Nancy may not come back to Larry and ask him just what he

Hints for Successful Communication with Nontechnical People

To communicate successfully, technical managers should always:

1. Give instructions in nontechnical terms, as much as possible
2. Avoid complicated explanations; *more* technical words don't increase nontechnical information
3. Get feedback to check understanding
4. Work at understanding why people act and react as they do

had in mind. Instead, she may guess, may think she knows, or may ask some other people. In any of the cases, there's a good chance that she will waste some time trying to find out. Even if she does decide to come back to Larry, she will still waste some time because she will not be able to do the job the way it was intended to be done from the first.

CONCLUSION

Finally, we need to look at another element that can well cause Larry some problems in dealing with nontechnical things and nontechnical people. Because Larry is a supervisor, it will be important for him to take a certain amount of supervisory training in order to understand how and why the people react. If the organization is at all progressive, it will see that Larry gets some proper training in supervision. He needs to learn some things about motivation, delegation, and com-

Attitudes for Successful Communication with Nontechnical People

To communicate successfully with nontechnical people, technical managers should understand that:

1. Nontechnical is not nonintelligent
2. Nontechnical people are equal contributors in organizational success
3. Complete accuracy in word usage is not a requirement for nontechnical understanding
4. Technical people need to develop nontechnical vocabularies

munications. He will have to learn how to handle poor performance, how to train employees, how to praise employees, how to counsel them, and how to do interviews. He will have to learn how to be perceptive enough to judge certain things and to make decisions about the best approach to use in handling employee problems.

As we will notice in the chapter on motivation (Chapter 8), this is certainly not an exact science. Some of the things that Larry is going to learn in his management training may strike him as being a waste of time, insignificant, or perhaps even incorrect. Because he won't be able to put behavior into a formula and because he won't be able to look it up in a reference book somewhere, he may decide that it's too inexact for his liking. He may react unfavorably by ignoring the training after he has had it; he may resort to mocking and ridiculing the instructor during the training; he may just have enough disgust for it that he will manage a way not to go. All of these are the wrong reactions. We have to sympathize with Larry because his whole background is one in which there are exact answers if one looks far enough. He is used to situations where answers can be predicted ahead of time and where the outcome was set by the specific action ahead of that. If Larry can learn to deal with people and handle people problems as they are, which is an inexact science, he will be a better supervisor; and if he can add tolerance to this, he will certainly be even better in dealing with nontechnical people.

Hints for Successful Communication with Nontechnical People

To communicate successfully, technical managers should always:

1. Give instructions in nontechnical terms, as much as possible
2. Avoid complicated explanations; *more* technical words don't increase nontechnical information
3. Get feedback to check understanding
4. Work at understanding why people act and react as they do

chapter four

How Can I Maintain a Positive Outlook in a Technical Environment?

INTRODUCTION

A technical environment can be a cloudy one—even a stormy one. Of course there are some storms that technical managers must simply ride out. But—even at that—there are things that they can do to make their own outlook a little sunnier. We deal with one of these, managing stress, in the next chapter. Here we deal with two others: technical managers' efforts to:

Combat stereotypes
Handle shifts in priorities

COMBAT STEREOTYPES

Where there's a stereotype, there's usually some fire. One marriage counselor in the Silicon Valley has made a career out of counseling couples (over 3000 so far) on the problems that result when one partner is an engineer, a scientist, or a computer whiz. The reason?

> The sci-tech personality is trained to collect data, assess it, spot flaws, and draw conclusions. He is very conservative, rigid, fearful of making a mistake. He hates conflicts and avoids them by adopting an air of detachment.

Unfounded bias? Well, just look at this dialogue from one case file:

Wife:	He doesn't understand feelings, just facts. The computer at home was the last straw.
Husband (after his wife left him):	Now I have more time to spend with my computer.

The counselor elaborates:

> It's hard to love an engineer-scientist. Sometimes it feels like loving your vacuum cleaner. It does the job. It is steady. It is reliable. But it doesn't dazzle. (Faber, 1984, p. 93)

There you have it: the rest of your organization may see your staff as conservative, rigid, fearful, evasive, detached automatons—in a word, vacuum cleaners. And each person who holds that stereotype probably has had just enough contact with technical people to reinforce some part of the stereotype. Each will be as confident as the blind person sent to "evaluate" an elephant. (The first blind person felt only the elephant's trunk and reported, "The elephant is very much like a snake." The second blind person felt only the elephant's side and contested, "Oh, no, the elephant is very much like a wall."

The third blind person felt only the elephant's leg and protested, "Not at all—the elephant is very much like a tree." The fourth felt only the elephant's tail and concluded, "You are all wrong: the elephant is very much like a rope!")

Of course, the results would be just as misleading if blind elephants were sent to "evaluate" a person. Technical people may have stereotypes about managers in the organization. And these stereotypes are just as important for the technical manager to combat.

Let's now go back to Matt Stephens in the research and development division. Janice Ashford, Matt's computer section chief, has been spearheading a project that has the attention of top management. Janice is always reluctant to release a project until it is "perfect." (Since perfect projects are rare, Janice rarely releases one without some nudging from Matt.) In this particular case, however, there really have been some

Combatting Stereotypes of Technical People

To tackle the stereotypes about technical and professional people, technical managers can:

1. View the stereotypes as the "working hypotheses" others have about their groups, and set out to change these stereotypes without taking them personally
2. Accumulate "points" for their group by taking part in high-visibility activities with their own supervisors and peers
3. Respond rationally to criticism
4. Know the "unwritten rules" and tell their people about them so the staff won't be caught off guard
5. Openly discuss the reality of dependence in the organization and the need for independence in their groups
6. Avoid "battles to the death"

tricky technical problems to iron out. Janice needs to talk face to face with Jim Swales, vice president of operations, to deal with his concern. Matt has repeatedly arranged for Jim and Janice to get together, but Jim has consistently canceled the meetings at the last minute. Now

Even though the project due date hasn't yet arrived, the company's president has expressed "eagerness" to see project results to Matt's supervisor, to Matt himself, and — when he has seen her in the hall—even to Janice. Janice's apparently cool response to his casual questions aroused his concern that something was amiss. He has hinted that Janice may not be a "team person" and asked—in an indirect way—if she has been a bottleneck in this project.

Matt's supervisor, Kenneth Beyers (vice president of science and engineering), is beginning to get nervous about project completion and put pressure on Matt. Ken has made several comments like: "We don't want the front office involved in this until the project's completed. Otherwise we'll have a solution imposed on us that will hurt us politically and disappoint us technically."

Matt knows that mention of the "front office" is Ken's way of signaling an alert. Ken usually delegates a task and then leaves it alone unless Matt calls him in. Historically, Ken has intervened only when a political bomb was about to drop. And the bombardier has usually been the vice president of operations, Jim Swales. Swales is a self-appointed rival of Ken Beyers. He sees Beyers's operation as "soft" and inefficient and seems annoyed by Beyers's consistently good record.

Janice is just plain angry. She's had to bite her tongue when the president has asked about the project. She's even ducked into a doorway several times to avoid coming face to face with him in the hall. She knows that she's in the right technically. She resents Swales inaccessibility. (She *knew* the man was a chauvinist all along; he's finally come out of the closet.) And she's irritated that Matt hasn't just told him off—or at least gotten out of her way so that she could do it.

What a spot! Matt feels caught in a squeeze. Whenever he feels the pressure mounting, he tries to find some time alone to "detoxify." And he speeds up detoxification when he reminds himself that most of the strong feelings surrounding him grow out of the *situation*: he isn't personally the *source* of them and he won't let himself be the *target* of them either. How can he refuse to be the target? Well, the less he acts like one, the less he'll be seen as one. (If he can't control other people's aim, he can at least control his own behavior.) He won't get defensive, angry, withdrawn, overly authoritative, or behave in the other ways that targets typically do. The president is right in guessing that *something* is wrong. He has supposed incorrectly that Janice is the problem. (Unfortunately, Janice's aloofness and anger make that supposition likely.) Like anyone else, he has "filled in the blanks" with only limited information. But his tentative conclusions are just that: tentative. He's open enough to revise them when he gets better information. But he needs to get new information while his conclusions are still tentative; and he needs to get it from Kenneth or from Matt, *not* from Jim Swales.

And Matt's informal access to the president will make getting that information to him possible. Formally, he has already built up some "points" for his group by being active in some successful, highly visible projects. He helped the president muster employee and community support for the United Fund, for example. And he's been much in demand as an industrial speaker to community groups. He ironed out some problems with blue-collar workers and averted unionization. Matt has made a point of being visible to key people two levels above him in the organization. In each case, Matt has performed capably. Perhaps even more important, he's also used the opportunity to speak casually but highly of the people who work for him. He has developed respect from those above him in the organization and from his peers. (Ironically, management researchers tell us that respect from higher-ups in an organization is a good predictor—perhaps even a prerequisite—of respect from subordinates.)

When Matt hears criticism of himself or of his group, he responds rationally—systematically, not impulsively. For example, when Ken—in a bad mood—exploded: "Why *can't* you get Janice off center? You expect me to work wonders with the front office when you can't even move your own employees off the dime!" Matt quietly acknowledged the truth in the statement: "We have had some unprecedented delays; and by the time I filled you in, the front office had already gotten concerned. That makes it tough to get the support of the front office." Then he simply kept quiet and let the conversation move on to another topic.

Later, when Ken had cooled off, Matt elaborated.

He acknowledged whatever truth was in the criticism	"We have had some unprecented delays. That makes it tough to get the support of the front office."
He explained the dilemma.	"But we have a real problem. Janice foresees some serious technical problems without input from Swales. And Swales has canceled three meetings at the last minute. Unless we get Swales's attention, we have to choose between the appearance of foot-

	dragging and the fact of releasing a program that we know is faulty."
He recommended a course of action.	"So I'd like your help in doing one of two things: (1.) Get the needed clarification of these points from Swales within the next business week, or (2) Let the front office know that our hands are tied until we get the needed information."

Not only did Matt see that needed information moved upward, he also saw to it that needed information reached Janice as well. For one thing, he needed to fill Janice in on some of the "unwritten rules" he had learned the hard way. Like many technical people, Janice is a literalist. She's likely to hear the words verbatim and be oblivious to the cues hidden among them. Of course, Matt won't approach any of his people with "another set of rules." But he can speak from his own experience; "In the past, whenever Ken has mentioned the 'front office,' it's signaled something afoot that he couldn't discuss in more detail. I've found from experience that he's usually preparing me for some kind of power squeeze. So I'm betting that more than our project is at stake; it will be important for us to watch for the signals as well as listen to the words."

And while he must respect her technical independence, Matt is open about Janice's organizational dependence on other people involved: she is dependent on others for pay, for access to the career ladder, and for cooperation on future projects.

As he talks with Janice, as he talks with Ken, as he thinks through the problem itself, Matt will be on guard for any behavior that might incite a "battle to the death." In fact, he may need to ignore direct challenges from Swales. In the past, he's done several things that kept battle lines from forming. (Things that, by the way, had a stereotype-shattering effect in and of themselves.)

1. *He's stated his case with facts, not with evaluative labels.* For example, if Swales charges that Matt is dragging his feet, *Matt will explain*:

> We need your input on these issues before we can go any further. Janice has made three appointments with you to discuss them, but you've canceled each appointment at the last minute.

Matt won't rise to the bait: "You've got that just exactly backwards, Jim: you're the one who won't cooperate!" (Note the difference between "canceled" and "won't cooperate.")

2. *He's dodged challenges (or threats) without returning them.* For example, when Swales has threatened to "ruin your chances with the front office," *Matt has simply ignored the outburst and let Swales continue to blow off steam. He hasn't returned the challenge:* "You'll ruin *my* chances! Not if you've got any sense: I can let some skeletons out of the closet myself, you know!"

3. *He has refused the temptation to "ambush" his adversaries.* When someone like Swales draws on his bag of dirty tricks, it's been hard to resist setting him up. *But Matt has consistently operated aboveboard.* True, an ambush might really give him some temporary satisfaction. But he's not willing to risk his reputation for being consistent and predictable. One study of "derailed" executives put it this way: "Some executives committed what is perhaps management's only unforgivable sin: They betrayed a trust. This rarely had anything to do with honesty, which was a given in almost all cases. Rather, it was a one-upping of others, or a failure to follow

through on promises that wreaked havoc in terms of organizational efficiency" (McCall & Lombardo, 1983, p. 28). That doesn't mean that Matt has been glib with information about his staff or his plans. It does mean that each step he's taken in handling a difficult situation has grown logically and systematically out of the previous one: he has not been a Dr. Jekyll/ Mr. Hyde.

Matt's battle against stereotypes has had a second front, too: his own employees have sometimes cast the department's relationship with top management in "them against us" terms. To combat unfair stereotypes of management, Matt has tried various approaches (see box).

It's easy from a distance to feel that people who have moved to the top (especially if they do it rapidly) have done so at the expense of others. It's easy to assume that for them the end justifies the means. Of course that may be true in some cases. But by and large, movement up the organizational ladder systematically weeds out people who don't deal fairly with others. In that study of executives who derailed on their way to the top, the most common cause of derailment was: "insensi-

Combatting Stereotypes about Management

To combat unfair stereotypes of management, technical managers can:

1. Distinguish between a strong career orientation and ruthlessness
2. Identify the conditions of conflict with management
3. Demonstrate the steady, systematic behavior that gives them credibility with their employees just as it does with higher management

tive to others: abrasive, intimidating, bullying style." Tied for second place were specific performance problems and such adjectives as: "overly ambitious: thinking of next job, playing politics." Tied for third were: "cold, aloof, arrogant," "betrayal of trust," and "overmanaging: unable to delegate or build a team."

Often a conflict between top management and Matt's employees has resulted from the structure of the organization. By definition, top management must concern itself with survival issues: competing for a larger share of the market, surviving changes (and increases) in federal regulation, withstanding attacks by consumer groups. And just as predictably, Matt's employees are more concerned about producing the best possible product. The difference in priorities was apparent, for example, when Matt's bid for money to purchase new equipment lost out to the public relations bid for a community service project. (At the time, the company's proposed new waste treatment plant was meeting stiff opposition by neighborhood groups.)

Matt's view of a situation has carried some weight with his employees because they've seen over time that he means what he says, that he does what he says, and that he exercises good judgment in what he says.

HANDLE SHIFTS IN PRIORITIES

Perhaps the greatest blows to Matt's outlook have come from abrupt shifts in priorities at the top. For example, Janice believed that some new equipment would help her speed up the needed research to make a product more competitive. She thought that she had people, equipment, money, and time lined up. Then a consumer group threatened a law suit

Handling Shifts in Priorities

To handle shifts in priorities, technical managers should:

1. Simply steel themselves for embarrassment
2. Tell other people involved as soon as possible and as straightforwardly as possible
3. Treat the disappointment of other people involved as they would any other important loss
4. Analyze the impact of the change and help make the needed adjustments

over the company's proposed waste treatment facility. The resources provided Janice were immediately recalled to give the public relations staff whatever they needed to head off court action. Janice felt set up, tricked, and abandoned. And Matt found it hard not to feel the same way.

Matt could more easily identify some things *not to do* than things to do. He knew it wouldn't help to pin the blame, to make excuses, or to blow up (all of which he felt like doing). What would have resulted from these negative behaviors?

Negative Behavior	Likely Result
Pin the blame on top management	Increase Janice's resentment
	Increase the frequency and intensity of the resulting behavior: sulking, avoiding contact, "blowing up"
Make excuses	Undermine his reputation for directness and honesty
	Create the impression that he didn't understand Janice's point of view

Blow up	Negate the example of interpersonal behavior that he's been trying to set for Janice
	Undermine his reputation for consistency and predictability

Deciding what *to do* was harder. He prepared himself for the embarrassment of breaking the news to Janice. And then he let her know as soon as he was certain of the change. He didn't sandwich the bad news in between gushes of flowery praise, he didn't disguise the news with a string of four-syllable words, he didn't delay telling her until she had heard it through the grapevine.

Matt treated Janice's loss like he would any other important loss (more in Chapter 15). First he just listened. And listened. Then he acknowledged Janice's disappointment, her embarrassment in front of her employees, and her hurt over feeling abandoned. Only then did he work with her to analyze the full impact of the shift in priorities and help her plan adjustment to her work load and to her priorities.

What might result from these positive behaviors?

Positive Behavior	Likely Result
Prepare himself for embarrassment	Act as an example that Janice could follow in dealing with her own employees
Let Janice know of change	Save Janice time and trouble in moving further in the wrong direction
	Strengthen this image as being direct and honest

Treat Janice's disappointment like any other important loss	Demonstrate real concern for Janice
Analyze impact and help make adjustment.	Provide antidote to "all or nothing" thinking

CONCLUSION

Two elements in the technical environment pose a real threat to a positive outlook. First, there are the endless stereotypes—those *about* technical and profession people and those *held by* technical and professional people. Second, there are the inevitable priority shifts that play havoc with programs and with morale.

Combatting Stereotypes of Technical People

To fight stereotypes about technical and professional people, technical managers can:

1. View the stereotypes as the "working hypotheses" others have about their group, and set out to change these stereotypes without taking them personally
2. Accumulate "points" for their group by taking part in high-visibility activities with their own supervisors and peers
3. Respond rationally to criticism
4. Know the "unwritten rules" and tell their people about them so the staff won't be caught off guard
5. Openly discuss the reality of dependence in the organization and the need for independence in their staff
6. Avoid "battles to the death"

Combatting Stereotypes about Management

To combat unfair stereotypes of management, technical managers can:

1. Distinguish between a strong career orientation and ruthlessness
2. Identify the conditions of conflict with management
3. Demonstrate the steady, systematic behavior that gives them credibility with their employees just as it does with higher management

Handling Shifts in Priorities

To handle shifts in priorities, technical managers should:

1. Simply steel themselves for embarrassment
2. Tell other people involved as soon as possible and as straightforwardly as possible
3. Treat the disappointment of other people involved as they would any other important loss
4. Analyze the impact of the change and help make the needed adjustments

Combatting these elements is a tough battle. But it can pay off in a sunnier outlook for the technical manager and for his or her staff.

chapter five

How Can I Manage the Stress?

INTRODUCTION

> But the present world is a different one. Grief, calamity, and evil cause inner bitterness . . . there is disobedience and rebellion. . . . Evil influences strike from early morning until late at night . . . they injure the mind and reduce its intelligence and they also injure the muscles and the flesh. (Benson, 1975, p. 11)

Is this a modern doctor's lament? No, it was written by a Chinese physician 4600 years ago, but it seems just as appropriate today.

Stress is built into technical management. Some of it comes from the conflicting demands of technical excellence and administrative allegiance. Some of it grows out of the need to compete for scarce resources. Some of it grows out of the very nature of being responsible for the work of others. And some of it grows out of personality conflict. The stress a technical manager experiences from most of these sources is likely to vary over time and under different circumstances. One source of stress is likely to remain constant: personality conflict. And the cost of unmanaged stress is high. In this country, medical science has virtually eliminated death by infectious disease. The big killers now are heart attack, cancer, and stroke. Two of these—heart attack and stroke—are clearly stress related. And evidence that the third—cancer—has a stress-related component is mounting (Albrecht, 1979, p. 32). The organizational costs of stress show up on the bottom line through missed profit opportunity, through the rising cost of employee benefits, through absenteeism, and through turnover. The personal costs show up in premature death, in poor physical health, in unhappiness, and in destructive coping strategies, such as heavy drinking, overeating, smoking, and use of drugs.

ORGANIZATIONAL COSTS OF STRESS

Since interpersonal conflict is such a constant source of stress, Matt's relationship with Wade Slocum would be a good one to illustrate various stress cost-containment techniques (see box). Remember our earlier description of Wade?

WADE SLOCUM, CHIEF OF NEW PRODUCT DEVELOPMENT
Wade is a brilliant, impatient man in his early 50s. He came to the company after retiring from the military. He was considered a high-achieving "renegade" in both military and civilian circles. He takes a strong stand on some controversial issues and seems to be unconcerned about the way he's seen by top management. In fact, he almost seems to view management as a necessary evil: he actually enjoys seeing management discomfort with his behavior. He is impatient with administrative paperwork and with the people who do it. He leaves behind him a trail of frayed nerves, anger, and—sometimes—

Containing the Organizational Costs of Stress

To contain the organizational costs of stress, technical managers can:

1. Allow themselves—and others—some emotional distance
2. Recognize that what they can observe and manage is *behavior,* not attitudes or values
3. Have a clear mental picture of how things would look if they looked "just right"
4. Plan a systematic course of action to cut their losses when necessary
5. Avoid waving "red flags"
6. Present ideas assertively but not aggressively

deep resentment. More than one excellent secretary has claimed Wade as the "reason for leaving" in an exit interview.

Allow Themselves—and Others—Some Emotional Distance

Like most people, Matt likes to be liked. He'd like to be held in high regard by those who work for him. Even when he's *had* to make some decisions Wade didn't like, Matt has tried to please Wade in their social/personal interaction. The trouble is that what pleases Wade one minute won't please him the next. On one occasion Matt's cheerful good morning has been answered with a smile; on others with a scowl. Matt has tried to identify a pattern: maybe Wade is just a "morning person." No, maybe he's just an "afternoon person." After testing every possibility through his treatment of Wade, Matt finally has put a little emotional distance between himself and Wade. He's learned to be a little less concerned about Wade's reaction to him. And he's more understanding of others who stay at arm's length. Matt doesn't like the distancing; but he's learned to accept it. He doesn't build barriers in the space between the two of them—he just leaves it alone.

How did Matt learn to "leave it alone"? First, he took a careful look at his own behavior. He found a pattern in that at least: whatever Wade's behavior toward him, Matt responded by approaching. (We're using *approach* here as a technical term: the emotional opposite of *withdraw* and the behavior to go with it.)

> Matt greeted, Wade smiled, Matt tried to open conversation, Wade withdrew.
>
> Matt greeted, Wade scowled, Matt tried to open conversation, Wade withdrew.

The squeaky wheel gets the grease; the cranky employee was getting the attention. Matt realized that he was accepting full responsibility for the relationship. Because of limited time, meanwhile, he was inadvertently turning a cold shoulder to employees who were eager for his input and his attentions. By necessity, he arrived at a policy decision about his relationship with Wade: he would greet Wade pleasantly. Now and then he would even invite conversation. But at Wade's first sign of withdrawal—unless there was an overriding business reason to the contrary—he would leave the conversation alone.

Recognize That What They Can Observe and Manage Is *Behavior,* Not Attitudes or Values

Let's look at some definitions.

Attitude. A disposition, an opinion, or a belief

Value. A deeply held belief or standard that remains fairly constant over a long period of time

We often hear managers complain:

> "His whole problem is a bad attitude."
>
> "My problems aren't any different from any other manager's: nobody knows the value of work these days."

But what effect can a manager really have on attitudes and values? The United States during the 1960s was a testing ground for efforts to change these things. The results? Disappointing.

> Social activists found attitudes between the races largely unchanged.
>
> Corporate activists found that "fade out" or even backsliding often followed their efforts to change attitudes through sensitivity training.

On the other hand, changes in law and in company policy *did* result in behavior change. Whether they had the "right attitude" about it or not, people opened up jobs and housing to different races. Corporations began providing more employee assistance.

Have attitudes changed two decades later? Well, there is substantial evidence that changed behavior *eventually* produced changed attitudes. But the indisputable facts *still* pertain only to behavior.

There is a clear relationship between satisfaction on the job and lowered rates of turnover. So Matt does have concern about Wade's attitude toward the work. And to the extent that he can, Matt continues to manage Wade's work environment to keep Wade coming back. (Remember our discussion of Maslow in Chapter 2?) But he realizes that Wade has had his disposition for a long time; a cheerful greeting from Matt in the morning simply isn't likely to change it.

But there is no direct relationship between Wade's job satisfaction and his performance on the job. So Matt can put Wade's attitude into perspective. He manages the environment to keep Wade coming back; but he realizes that Wade has ultimate control over his own attitude, so he doesn't turn changing Wade's attitude into a "cause." He manages the job itself to influence Wade's performance. And it's Wade's *performance* that Matt will make an issue of if necessary.

Have a Clear Mental Picture of How Things Would Look if They Looked "Just Right"

The technical term for "using your imagination" is *visionary analysis*.

All of us at one time or another have fallen into this trap: we use all our energy fighting (and complaining about) the things that are wrong, but we commit little or no energy to developing a clear picture of how things could be right. Too often, in fact, we don't know it when we see it! We've said that Matt should put Wade's abrasiveness into perspective. But if his mental picture of a dismal relationship with Wade becomes *too* well developed, he may be blind to the slight gesture of reconciliation that Wade *might* make. If Matt accepts the mental picture of repeated failure in dealing with Wade without developing a counteractive mental picture of success with Wade, he may never see some slight change in behavior on his own part that might make a difference. He might even advance in Wade's mind the picture of Matt as an ineffective supervisor.

Here's the procedure we recommended to Matt right after an unsatisfactory exchange with Wade, an exchange that left Matt feeling angry (especially at himself), frustrated, and inadequate. This procedure helped Matt prepare emotionally to handle his next contact with Wade both competently and confidently.

1. Picture the next exchange with Wade going the way you want.
2. Ask yourself:
   a. How do I know that things are going well?
   b. How do I feel?
   c. Where are we?
   d. What am I wearing?
   e. What can I taste and smell?
   f. What do I say that shows things are going well?
3. Then write down a detailed description of the answer to these questions.

In effect, we asked Matt to mentally rehearse his next contact with Wade—rehearse it so well that he was aware of every detail he would see, taste, smell, feel, and say. After seeing himself succeed time and time again in his mental rehearsal, Matt had the confidence and the energy to deal with Wade yet another time.

Plan a Systematic Course of Action to Cut Their Losses When Necessary

Until now, Matt has continuously absorbed Wade's aggression for the sake of the organization. He constantly weighs the value of Wade's technical ability to the organization against the cost of Wade's abrasiveness to the organization. Losing Wade could really cost: competitors would pay top price for his ability and experience. But keeping Wade is costing, too. Matt knows that he may reach the point of diminishing returns. He may adopt the folk maxim, "A wink is as good as a nod to a blind horse." If Wade is a blind horse, he won't notice when Matt:

Winks

Nods

Does cartwheels and handstands

Falls into a frustrated, exhausted heap

Matt simply won't let things go that far. Once Matt is convinced that the cost of keeping Wade exceeds the cost of losing him, Matt will fire Wade. Until then, Matt somehow needs to limit his investment in Wade in order to deal fairly with the needs of other employees.

Matt has several investments to consider:

His time

His effort

His thoughts

His feelings

Matt has spent hours consoling Wade, hours persuading Wade, hours listening to Wade. If these investments show no result over a period of time, Matt will need to limit them.

How can any manager know when to stop? Well, of course, there's never any way to be certain that the very next encounter wouldn't have made a difference. But we believe three full-scale attempts to deal with the same issue is a reasonable limit. We wouldn't impose that limit: sales experts tell us that many substantial sales are made on the sixth call or after. But we do feel that unless Matt sets some reasonable limit, he'll be spending good time after bad: he'll be investing his time where there is a slim chance of a return and ignoring possible high-yield investments in other employees. After Matt has dealt with a given issue three times, we'd suggest that he do one of two things:

Withdraw from further discussion, *or*

Put the original issue aside and deal with the underlying one: the stress between them and the lack of progress they are making

Matt's investment of time is, of course, hand in hand with his investment of effort. But effort is worth additional consideration. For example, suppose that Matt has delegated full authority to Wade on a particular project. (That's Matt's preferred management style.) Wade's decisions have overstepped his bounds and, as a result, he has alienated almost every other project member. Three times Matt has discussed the situation with Wade; three times he has been convinced that Wade understood and accepted what was expected; three times he has been disappointed. Allowing Wade full authority is demanding too much of Matt's energy. In the next meeting, Matt will withdraw some authority: he will consult with Wade, but Matt himself will make the major decisions. If this strategy fails after three attempts, Matt will withdraw even more authority: he may try to win Wade's support, but he won't

Matt gave his preferred style *(join)* his best effort three times.

Then he retreated to his first backup style: *consult*.

Next he retreated even further to his second backup style: *sell*.

Finally, Matt retreated to his least preferred style: *tell*.

Employee Input

rely on Wade for much input. If the selling effort fails three times, Matt will withdraw yet more authority: he will simply tell Wade what to do.

Step by step, Matt would systematically withdraw the investment medium: in this instance—his energy and Wade's authority. What would decreased authority do to Wade's effectiveness on the job? Undoubtedly that would decrease, too. How about his job satisfaction? Undoubtedly the same. Perhaps for the first time, Wade would be experiencing the consequences of his own behavior more keenly than Matt. And careful, malice-free management of consequences is Matt's strongest tool in dealing with any problem employee.

Matt has invested a disproportionate amount of thought in Wade as well. He's had Wade on the brain as he drove to work, as he drove home, as he took a coffee break, as he ate lunch—even as he talked with other employees. Habits are hard to break, and breaking this habit of thought will be harder than most. But when he decides that it's important to his success with other employees, Matt will consciously begin to substitute other subject matter when thoughts of Wade dominate. When his thoughts wander, "I surely hope Wade will turn this thing around," he will consciously redirect them: "I need to get back with Janice today to see if she's made any progress with the operations staff."

Probably the hardest habit for Matt to break will be his habit of investing emotion in Wade. It seems sometimes that Matt cares more about Wade's success than Wade himself does. Matt has run the risk of accepting more responsibility for Wade's feelings and behavior than Wade himself. Perhaps that would be admirable in a crisis; but as a chronic condition it can seriously limit Matt's ability to manage consequences—and therefore limit his ability to manage period. Even in a crisis, the lifeguard instructor's advice rings true: "Rule number one: Don't let the person you're trying to save pull you under!"

Avoid Waving Red Flags

It's actually easier to figure out what *not to do* in his relationship with Wade than to figure out what *to do.* The obvious things not do do are losing his temper, using abusive language, making unfounded accusations. But there are other things to avoid:

Blaming Wade for Matt's Own Feelings. Matt won't explode, "You make me so angry by walking off like that!" Instead, Matt will accept responsibility for his own feelings, "When you walk off before I've finished talking, I feel angry and frustrated." The difference between blame and action/reaction is a subtle one when you see it dispassionately. But in the heat of a conflict, it can make the difference between escalation and detente.

Labeling Facts as Facts. Matt won't fall into the trap of presuming omniscience: "You just want to give me a hard time because I couldn't get the money for that new equipment you wanted." Instead, he'll label feelings as feelings: "Sometimes I feel that our relationship is strained because you're upset over not getting that new equipment."

Denying the Truth. In a heated conflict even the most zealous combatant hangs his or her accusations on a thread of truth. And Wade knows which truth hurts the most. But Matt will be on his guard not to deny any fragment of the truth even when it is presented as part and parcel of numerous inaccuracies—or even lies. Matt consistently tries to either ignore them or simply acknowledge them matter of factly.

Present Ideas Assertively but Not Aggressively

Most of us grew up with the uneasy feeling that in a conflict there were only two choices: victim or villain. And neither role is a very satisfying one. Most people that we've asked say they feel these things when they've allowed themselves to be the victim of a conflict:

Depressed
Discouraged
Stupid
Frustrated
Angry
Guilty

When we've asked how they've felt when they themselves have been the villains, they've said:

Depressed
Discouraged
Stupid
Frustrated
Angry
Guilty

What we've somehow missed is a way to take care of ourselves without clobbering anyone else. Not a piece of cake. But two psychologists, Barbara Winship and Jan Kelley (1976), have given us a model that we've used successfully many times.

1. First, establish some common ground. Summarize the *other person's* point of view in your own words.
2. Next, let your listener know that you're changing directions. Use a connecting word, such as *but* or *therefore.*

3. Third, summarize the situation as *you* see it.
4. Then let your listener know there's more to come. Use a connecting word, such as *so* or *therefore.*
5. Finally—make your request, refuse a request, or "set something straight."

For example, in a conversation with Wade, Matt might say:

> I know you'd like to forget about Janice and her problems. You've got work load enough in your own section. But we run the risk of late charges on this project for XYZ if we can't solve this software problem. And since Jim Swales is virtually unavailable, your input is critical. You've got more operations experience than anyone else in the division. So I want you to get with Janice by close of business today and commit an hour of your time to her by the end of this week.

PERSONAL COSTS OF STRESS

Not only is it important that Matt contain the organizational costs of stress, it is equally important that he contain the personal costs as well.

Several years ago Matt felt he was hanging by a thread. He was becoming compulsive about work: even if a given course of action was seeming unproductive, he would pour more and more time and energy into it. Without realizing it, he was working longer and longer hours and getting less and less done. But somehow the only solution seemed to work yet more. He was relieving tension at work by smoking an occasional (at least in the beginning) cigarette. (That surprised even Matt: he had some respiratory allergies, and he had never liked to be in the same room with smokers!) And he was raiding the snack machine more and more often. In a period of six months he had gained about 15 pounds. His wife and children were upset about his late hours—especially since he often forgot to let them know he wouldn't be home in time for dinner. He would just pick up a burger, some fries, and a milkshake at the place across the street. When he finally did get home, he felt such tension in the air that his "little drink at bedtime" had turned to three or four. And he certainly couldn't waste time jogging or playing tennis anymore: he needed to put in every possible minute at work. He was on the verge of quitting his job and his marriage: he just didn't seem to have the energy to do any more. And it would take more to straighten out the mess at work and to keep his wife happy.

When he finally went to the company physician and complained about fatigue, Doc insisted that Matt take the time for a complete physical. The results weren't encouraging:

His blood pressure had risen since his last physical.

The serum cholesterol level in his blood had risen.

His weight gain put him over the acceptable range for his age and height.

Probably because of his smoking, he registered decreased lung capacity.

Since he was getting no regular exercise, it was no surprise that his pulse rate had gone up.

In fact, Doc said Matt was in a high-risk zone for five of the top correlates of longevity:

Blood pressure

Serum cholesterol level

Weight range

Containing the Personal Costs of Stress

To contain the personal cost of stress, technical managers can:

1. Use deep-breathing exercises and muscle relaxation exercises at intervals during a high-stress day to help reduce the physical and emotional wear and tear
2. Practice deep-breathing and muscle relaxation exercises at home *regularly*
3. Participate regularly in an aerobic exercise such as biking or swimming
4. Get ample sleep
5. Eat nutritiously and moderately
6. Give themselves verbal mental encouragement

Smoking

Regular exercise

In a word, Doc said Matt was a good candidate for heart attack or stroke. Doc believed a poor stock of stress management techniques was at the root of his problem. Admittedly, Matt had thought that all this stress management stuff was a fad—just a hangover from all that touchy-feely stuff we went through in the sixties. But Doc made no bones about it (excuse the pun): Matt's health was on the line. And that made all the difference. Matt made a serious search of the stress-management literature and found that certain techniques were mentioned consistently by a wide range of health specialists (see box).

Before undertaking this or any other program that represents a change from an established pattern, we suggest following Matt's lead: a complete physical and a go-ahead from a doctor before proceeding.

Use Deep-Breathing and Muscle Relaxation Exercises at Home Regularly

No one would expect to win tennis matches on the weekend without practicing the swings during the week. And no one *should* expect to win over stress in a crisis without practicing the "swings" regularly, either: the key to beating the monumental stresses is good practice at handling the daily ones. In Matt's case, he thought he was ignoring the "small stuff." But the stresses were taking a toll mentally and physically; he was actually only ignoring the danger signals. Often during the day Matt would feel the muscle at the back of his neck tighten up. He might rub his neck unconsciously—but otherwise he would pay no heed. Until he had a killer headache, that is. Then he tried to mollify it with super-strength aspirin. Before long, too much aspirin was giving him an upset stomach, so he began to use some Valium a doctor had prescribed a friend. Whatever he used, his strategy was the same: appease the Headache God and ignore his body.

In fact, Matt's body was asking for help of a different kind —for relaxation. Another person's body might make the same request a different way: an upset stomach, tightness in the chest, clammy hands. Regardless of the specific medium, the message is the same: *Time out!* When Doc finally translated the message for him, Matt had several choices:

Ignore it (until his body makes a life-threatening demand for attention) and live with the headaches.

Mask it with drugs so that he won't be bothered with the headaches. (That way he might even be able to ignore the life-threatening demands.)

Satisfy it with some time out.

Matt chose to satisfy it with time out. And he was pleased to learn that he didn't need to take a vacation to get it. He could give his body daily breaks by setting aside 20 minutes a day for deep-breathing and muscle relaxation exercises. Since he is a morning person, he found these exercises a good way to start off the day. To begin with, he used the same deep breathing exercise that we have found so helpful (Laird & House, 1984, p. 105). He would:

Breathe in to the count of 3.

Hold his breath for the count of 12.

Exhale for the count of 6.

Repeat the sequence three times. When he exhaled the third time, he pushed as much air out of his lungs as he possibly could.

After this beginning breathing exercise, Matt followed a sequence of tensing and relaxing the various muscle groups as he continued to breath deeply. He had recorded the detailed instructions in *Asserting yourself* (Bower & Bower, 1976, pp. 231–237). Then he let the tape talk him through the sequence —he didn't even think about that. After a week or so, he found that the sequence became almost automatic and he was free to concentrate on something pleasant or something neutral. (In *The relaxation response,* 1975, p. 114, Herbert Benson suggests the numeral 1.)

Use Deep-Breathing Exercises and Muscle Relaxation Exercises at Intervals during a High-Stress Day

Matt found his morning time out energizing. He felt that he had more mental energy and more physical energy as well. So he decided to allow himself some mini-time out when he was facing a high-stress situation at work. At home it was easier to satisfy two of the conditions for relaxation—a quiet environment and a comfortable position. But the other two conditions—a mental device and a passive attitude—were definitely portable (Benson, 1975, pp. 112–113). So even if he could manage only a two- or three-minute retreat, he would close his office door before he headed for a high-stress meeting and at least practice his deep-breathing exercise. If he had more time, he would even complete a deep muscle relaxation exercise. After awhile, he found he could even use deep breathing to clear his mind on the spot under fire. He just modified the last "exhale" in the sequence so that it wasn't noticeable to others.

Get Ample Sleep

Sleep is another way to give the body some time out. Matt insisted that his children get adequate sleep to be in good form for school. But until Doc reminded him, he had forgotten that ample sleep would also improve his form for work.

Participate Regularly in Aerobic Exercise, such as Biking or Swimming.

Lack of exercise is one of the traditional explanations of the rise in frequency of heart attacks and strokes (Benson, 1975, p. 15). As relaxation is important, so is regular and moderate exertion. What Matt had been getting was irregular and strenuous. After getting virtually no exercise for months, he would occasionally accept a friend's challenge to tennis and then spend a whole day on the courts. After several weeks of relaxation exercises, after several weeks of adequate sleep, Matt found that he had the energy to schedule a brisk walk into his daily routine. Over a period of time he found that his capacity for exertion had increased and he was troubled less and less by fatigue.

Eat Nutritiously and Moderately

Matt really hadn't been doing either one. He had been consuming hamburgers, french fries, and milkshakes to the point of almost painful overstuffing. Not only was he eating too much (and putting on weight), he was also eating foods high in calories, salt, sugar, fat, and additives. And his increased alcohol consumption was simply adding empty calories with no nutritional value at all. Doc suggested that all that eating and drinking was a pretty unhealthy attempt to fight off tension. And he suggested that Matt look at one of the excellent books now available as a guide to filling, nutritious food:

Foods for healthy kids by Lendon Smith. New York: McGraw-Hill, 1981.

Laurel's kitchen by Laurel Robertson, Carol Flinders, & Bronwen Godfrey. Petaluma, CA: Nilgiri Press, 1976.

The Pritikin program for diet and exercise by Nathan Pritikin with Patrick M. McGrady, Jr. New York: Grosset and Dunlap, 1979.

Smith (p. 62) had the same advice in reaction to all the conditions listed below—"Stop sugar."

Insomnia
Feeling aggressive, surly, or noncompliant; having a chip on your shoulder
Being sick too much

Pritikin had this to say about fat (p. 9):

Of the calories that we Americans consume, about 40 or 45 percent come in the form of fats. Many health authorities recommend cutting this down to about 30 percent. We feel that fats are so bad for you that you should eat no more than 5 to 10 percent fat.

Essentially, fats do three kinds of damage. First of all, they suffocate your tissues by depriving them of oxygen. Second, they raise the level of cholesterol and uric acid in your tissues, contributing to atherosclerosis and gout. Third, they impede carbohydrate metabolism and foster diabetes. . . .

In one clinical experiment, fourteen heart patients suffering from angina pectoris drank a glass of heavy cream after an overnight fast. Within five hours, their blood became six times cloudier than normal and, though they had been at rest during this entire procedure, most of them suffered a severe angina attack within minutes of each other. Normally angina strikes only under the stress of strenuous physical activity. But the fats had deprived the heart of enough oxygen—just as exertion might have.

When this test was repeated with a *fat-free* drink containing the same calories and volume, *no* angina attacks or abnormalities occurred!

Robertson et al. had this to say about overweight (p. 335):

Probably the largest single health hazard of middle-age obesity is maturity-onset (middle age) diabetes. This type of diabetes often responds dramatically to weight reduction. In one large study 75 percent of the diabetics of this type who achieved their desired weight had their blood sugar levels return to normal. . . .

Also closely associated with obesity is high blood pressure or hypertension, and half of them are unaware of it. One-fifth to one-third of all hypertensive adults in the United States are markedly overweight. These people have more illnesses and

> earlier deaths and run an especially greater risk of heart disease than either hypertensive people who are not obese or obese people who are not hypertensive. . . .
>
> Excess weight increases the work load of the cardiovascular system. Consequently, though it is not true for all, the blood pressure of many people goes down when they lose weight. Weight loss also improves the life expectancy of people who have had heart attacks, and often favorably affects angina pectoris or heart pains. There is also a significant association between obesity and gall bladder disease, especially in women, but in this case losing weight does not improve the condition once it has developed.

Fortunately, each of these authorities had some suggestions about satisfying, tasty substitutes for his high-calorie, high-salt, high-sugar, high-fat, high-additive standbys. Matt was able to find others in any of the latest Weight Watchers cookbooks from the local bookstore.

Give Themselves Verbal Mental Encouragement

That's right! Doc advised him to talk to himself! According to Doc [and to psychologist Albert Ellis, Ellis & Harper, 1975)], everyone is pressured by little voices in their heads that say things like:

> If Swales isn't completely satisfied with this, I'll have a nervous breakdown.
>
> If I have to look at those drawings one more time, I'll go crazy!
>
> If Ken doesn't back me up on this, my career will be ruined!

When Doc asked Matt if he heard high-pressure voices like that in his head, Matt's only reply was, "How much time do you have, Doc?"

Doc's advice sounded crazier to him than the little voices: "Substitute a manageable word for the overwhelming word of the high-pressure voice. Then talk back to it." But Matt promised to give it a try. Several days later he was headed to Ken's office for a hot-and-heavy discussion. As he walked down the hall he heard that little voice shriek: "If Ken doesn't back me up on this, my career will be ruined!" Silly as he felt, he replied (not out loud, though that wouldn't have done any harm): "No, I won't be *ruined,* I'll just be *disappointed.*"

Can you believe it? He actually felt better, more confident. It's the most effective antidote we've found for what some psychologists call "catastrophyzing." (We call it making the worst out of a good situation.)

CONCLUSION

Stress is built in to technical management. And it exacts a high cost from an organization as well as a high cost from individuals. Organizational costs show up in missed profit opportunity, in soaring costs of employee benefits, in absenteeism, in turnover. Individual costs show up in premature death, in poor physical health, in unhappiness, and in destructive coping strategies, such as heavy drinking, overeating, snacking, and use of drugs.

The stresses won't take care of themselves. Even the small ones can accumulate and cause serious harm if they are ignored. Fortunately, the technical manager can take positive steps to manage them.

Containing the Organizational Costs of Stress

To contain the organizational costs of stress, technical managers can:

1. Allow themselves—and others—some emotional distance
2. Recognize that what they can observe and manage is *behavior,* not motives or attitudes
3. Have a clear mental picture of how things would look if they looked "just right"
4. Plan a systematic course of action to cut their losses when necessary
5. Avoid waving "red flags"
6. Present ideas assertively but not aggressively

Containing the Personal Costs of Stress

To contain the personal cost of stress, technical managers can:

1. Use deep-breathing exercises and muscle relaxation exercises at intervals during a high-stress day to help reduce the physical and emotional wear and tear
2. Practice deep-breathing and muscle relaxation exercises at home *regularly*
3. Participate regularly in an aerobic exercise such as biking or swimming
4. Get ample sleep
5. Eat nutritiously and moderately
6. Give themselves verbal mental encouragement

chapter six

How Can I Build a Technical Team?

INTRODUCTION

Lord Glendower: I can call the spirits from the vasty deep.
Hotspur: But will they come . . . ?
(Shakespeare, *Henry IV*)

At one time, Matt Stephens' outlook wasn't much different from the overconfident Glendower's: "I'll rate performance, I'll authorize pay," he thought. "So *I* can tell *them* what to do!" Now an experienced manager, a more down-to-earth Matt looks back and laughs to himself: "But will they do it?"

If telling were only enough, Matt's job would have been a snap. But it hasn't been that easy. More than once, Matt has watched a project teeter on the edge of disaster while individuals displayed their individual talents to best advantage (or withheld their talents to best advantage, as the case might be). He worked hard to find a way to direct their energies into a single group effort.

A way was the stuff Matt's dreams were made of. But he did find *some ways*—some specific methods—that moved teamwork out of the realm of make-believe and into the realm of reality.

Matt's guiding principle is flexibility. At one time or another, being an effective manager has required him to use each of the "standard" management styles: telling, selling, consulting, and joining. Of course Matt has a preferred way of operating which he relies on unless certain variables make a shift in style appropriate: variables in the organization, in his staff, or in the task itself. Matt is consistent, but he's not boxed in.

Matt knows that project delays will result if his employees fail to pull into a team. In fact, that's why he was put in this job. His own supervisor expected him to turn an assortment of technocrats into a well-coordinated team. To see how he continues to do that, let's see how Matt interacts with some members of his staff.

Stan Kettles, a bright young computer specialist, would make a textbook example of the "absentminded professor." Stan knows a lot and he's perfectly willing to share what he knows. But listeners often walk away in a daze.

Joyce Jenrette, Matt's secretary, is almost too good to be true. She's well organized, quick, and capable. But her efficiency sometimes comes across as abruptness. In fact, most of the rest of Matt's staff seem a little intimidated by her.

Shelley Bourne, project management section chief, is an outstanding engineer. She began in the drafting department and worked her way through school as she moved up in the company. She has a phenomenal ability to make sense out of a jumble of data—she's a terrific organizer. But in her zest for organization she sometimes bulldozes other people's ideas and feelings without realizing it.

Larry Douglass, chief of product refinement, is Matt's most experienced engineer. He is probably also Matt's most skillful "people person." But Larry sometimes accepts too much responsibility for others—tries too hard to cover for their mistakes or take up the slack on their off days.

John Eppsinger, chief of planning and scheduling, is a young engineer right out of a prestigious university. He's a loner. He seems to resist being "brought up to date" on a project by any other staff member.

Roger Fuller, the senior budget specialist, is bright and quick. But Matt sometimes feels that he has to play "Twenty Questions" to get the information he wants. For some reason, Roger seems to be holding back.

TASK ORIENTATION AND PERSON ORIENTATION

Matt's ability to shift from task orientation to person orientation (or person orientation to task orientation) has enabled him to work well with a variety of people, a variety of tasks, and a variety of organizational conditions.

Matt's people are different; and he must approach them differently to get the results he wants. Nine times out of ten when Matt is interacting with his secretary, Joyce, he needs to give her only minimum direction about a task. Then, as far as the task is concerned, Joyce is on "automatic." With Joyce, Matt's major investment of time and energy goes toward encouraging and maintaining Joyce's membership in his larger technical team. Matt sees to it that Joyce knows what's going on with his technical staff and that his technical staff know Joyce's role in the operation of the division. With Joyce, Matt's management behavior is largely person oriented.

But often when Matt initiates contact with Larry Douglass, chief of product refinement, the subject of conversation is task oriented. Larry is probably the best "people person" on Matt's staff. In fact, he sometimes gets too involved in personal issues. He has a tendency to overload himself by picking up the slack for an employee who's going through a crisis. Under those circumstances deadlines tend to slip. Matt doesn't ignore the personal issues important to Larry and his group, but he must often guide them back to task-oriented issues.

The tasks in Matt's division vary widely in complexity, in predictibility, and in urgency. When a task is either very simple or very complex with predictable outcomes, Matt finds his staff open to a direct, task-oriented approach: if Matt chooses a suitable delegation style, they don't seem to mind so much being told what to do. (We'll get into the nuts and bolts of delegation style in Chapter 9.) And when the task is urgent, they seem to welcome as much direction as Matt can give. But if a task is moderately complex or very complex with unpredictable outcomes, Matt finds that his people do best when he backs off from the task itself and helps the group maintain itself as a team.

In some instances, Matt has no choice. When management and union officials agreed on a parking assignment system that was inconvenient for most of Matt's staff, he had to inform his staff of the new rules. And if any person on his staff violated the agreement, he had no choice but to direct compliance. He saw no point in going through the motions of making a group decision; the decision had already been made by top management. When he has considered the other person involved, the task itself, and the conditions in the overall organization, Matt can choose to:

Tell. Make the decision himself and simply pass it on to his staff.

Sell. Make the decision himself and try to win the support of his staff.

Flexible Management

Technical managers can build team cooperation by following the guidelines for *flexible* (not *formula*) management:

1. Notice how each employee works best: when each works best on a task with close direction; when each works best with little direction on the task, but with support in coordinating teamwork
2. Distinguish between tasks that require close direction and those that do not
3. Identify organizational conditions that require close direction and those that do not
4. Be familiar with several interaction models that can be adapted to suit their own personalities and a given situation

Consult. First, get the maximum input from his staff, then make the decision himself.

Join. Get maximum input from the group and let the group make the decision.

To be sure that he practices *flexible* management, not *formula* management, Matt can do several things (see box).

INTERACTION MODELS

These are some of the models that Matt has used successfully in the past.

Tell

When a task is either very simple or very difficult with predictable outcomes, employees are often happy to have a direct, step-by-step explanation of what's expected. Sometimes that's what an inexperienced employee needs. And if there is a tested step-by-step procedure for a lengthy or complicated task, there's no need to require even experienced employees to reinvent the wheel when they take on something new. If they can improve on the old procedure, fine: but their manager can at least give them the benefit of the information on hand.

Sometimes a checklist is all that's necessary. Even fairly complicated tasks can be presented simply in a two-column checklist, such as this:

What to do	How to do it
Record payments due.	Record amount of check, check number, payment code, and date on second line for each vendor.
	Total payments due for the month on line 34 of budget record.
Calculate balance after payments.	Record beginning balance on line 35. Subtract total payments due. Record ending balance on line 36.

For some tasks telling involves showing as well—especially with new employees. A manager may need to use the old World War II formula for giving instructions:

Tell the employee what to do

Show the employee what to do

Let the employee do it himself or herself

Review the task with the employee

When the purpose of telling is to clarify expectations, this approach can be a good one:

1. Spell out expectations. ("I'd like the work to get done well and get done on time. I believe we could meet both those goals if you notified me right away of any schedule slippage, however slight.")
2. *Acknowledge What's Going Well Now.* ("As things stand now, your work quality is excellent.")
3. Identify what's not going well now. ("But several projects have been late.")
4. Point out the advantages of doing things the way you want. ("If you notify me before the close of business on the day you notice any schedule slippage, there's a good chance we can allocate more staff or adjust peak work periods to avoid missing a deadline.")
5. Spell out the consequences of noncompliance. ("If you don't notify me right away, it may be impossible to make any adjustments in time. Then we will be faced with late fines that can eat up our profit.")

Sell

The decision to use a selling approach has little to do with the complexity of the task. More than likely, it results from some other factor—the personalities involved, the organizational conditions, or the urgency of the task.

With some employees, Matt *sells* instead of *tells* because they are likely to withhold support for projects they didn't originate. Unless, that is, they recognize some personal advantage to themselves. Some supervisors tell us that working around this NIH (Not Invented Here) syndrome is one of the most frustrating parts of their jobs. Matt often uses a selling approach with John Eppsinger, the young chief of planning and scheduling. Matt doesn't mislead John about who made the original decision—Matt himself or higher management. But through his behavior, Matt acknowledges that there's one decision that only John can make: the decision to give support or to withhold it. Even a decision that's "cast in stone" can be hampered or discredited without the support of key people. Military supervisors have told us countless horror stories about arrogant young commissioned officers who "washed out" because they failed to win the support of seasoned "chiefs" (chief petty officers) who reported to them. Each of those horror stories has, we believe, a civilian counterpart.

Sometimes organizational conditions require that Matt sell an idea or approach when he would really prefer to get more input from his people. Matt may even ask his employees to support a decision by top management that he himself has fought wholeheartedly. It's an uncomfortable situation at best. But once the decision is made and publicly announced, Matt gives it the opportunity to work and encourages his staff to do the same. For one thing, Matt wants to be sure he doesn't hamper progress with the NIH syndrome himself. For another, Matt's opposition would make him a top contender for scapegoat unless his efforts to make the decision work are apparent to everyone. (Ideally, of course, the scapegoat's job has been abolished permanently. But when the pressure has been great and a misfired program has been visible, we've seen it reappear ad hoc with little or no warning.)

Occasionally the urgency of a situation requires that Matt sell an idea. Matt generally plans well enough to get input before a situation becomes urgent. But when such a situation does occur he'll *sell* instead of *tell* if at all possible so that he can benefit from the added support that's likely to result.

How does Matt sell an idea to an employee? Let's use a recent conversation with John to illustrate.

First, Matt explained the benefits of the idea to John. "The new reporting procedure will speed up the distribution of revised schedule information—especially to the shops."

Next, he spelled out the features of the new procedures. "In the procedure, a planner will modify or replace the control cards as before. But in addition, his assistant will code information into the terminal and transmit it to the shop as well."

Finally, he spelled out just what John and his staff needed to do in order to enjoy the benefits. "You'll need to schedule each planner and each planner assistant to go to one of five two-hour briefings next week. I know that you hate to lose the time and you may even need to schedule some overtime as a result. But the potential time savings is great. And the improved data flow to the shop should eliminate avoidable downtime. So I hope you and your staff will give it your best effort."

Consult

Often Matt needs input from his people to get a clear picture of a situation. It may be that his employees are "on the front line" of a situation and Matt isn't. Or it may be that the situation involves specialized knowledge that Matt simply doesn't have himself. If Matt wants to get maximum input but retain control of related decisions, he uses a consulting approach.

The job instruction for new engineers several years ago is a good illustration. That year, Matt hired three competent but inexperienced engineers right out of college. He teamed each with a senior engineer for on-the-job training: one in planning and scheduling, one in project management, and one in product refinement. Before long the frustration level of each person closely involved became almost intolerable. The new engineers said they were learning nothing. They were being abandoned with a stack of manuals written in gobbledygook. The senior engineers said the new ones were still "wet behind the ears." They just weren't catching on and were taking up a lot of time asking the same questions over and over again.

In the midst of the angry complaints he was getting, Matt had trouble getting specific information about exactly what was going on. In this case, he decided to consult with the individuals involved one at a time rather than as a group. In cases where emotion hasn't run so high, however, he has consulted a small group with equally good results.

With each individual, Matt followed this consulting model. He was careful to:

1. *Check Each Person's Understanding of the Problem.* Usually, Matt just made a simple statement to get the conversation going, such as "The job instruction program seems to be causing some problems." Then he kept quiet to give the other person time to think and speak at his or her own pace. In only one case, the engineer remained speechless after over a minute of silence. So Matt encouraged him with the open question, "How do you see the problem?"
2. *Clarify Each Person's Role in Arriving at a Solution.* Matt didn't disguise the fact that he intended to make the final decision about what would be done. In fact, he made it clear that although he needed to decide what changes to make, he wanted to be sure he understood the problem and had full input from everyone before he did anything.
3. *Develop Criteria for a Good Solution.* Matt asked each person what characteristics a "good solution" would need to have. He wrote down each suggestion whether he agreed with it or not.
4. *Encourage Data and Idea Sharing.* Matt didn't present any preconceived ideas about what would solve the

problem. He simply listened to each person's ideas and took careful notes. He made *no* evaluative remarks during this period of sharing. Generating ideas is a creative process; evaluating is a restrictive one. Being creative and evaluative at the same time is like stepping on the accelerator and the brakes simultaneously. During this sharing with his employees, Matt learned of a number of problems that jeopardized the instruction program: senior engineers had no work load relief while they were doing training; they had no authorized overtime; they had no training on how to do training.

5. *Summarize Each Person's Ideas to His or Her Satisfaction.* Several times Matt found that he had misunderstood someone's ideas. When he summarized—without inserting his own opinion—his employees clarified just what they had meant to get across.
6. *Evaluate.* After Matt had talked to all the employees involved, he compiled the criteria and evaluated suggestions.
7. *Decide.* Matt reached a decision, and then told each involved employee about it. Again, if the situation had been less emotional, he could have chosen to announce his plan to the whole group at one time.

Join

Sometimes Matt believes that a decision can best be made by the group itself. Administratively, of course, Matt is held responsible for whatever goes on in his division, and he doesn't use participative decision making in an effort to dodge that responsibility. But there are times when an informed technical decision can best be made by the technical specialists themselves. When that's the case, Matt helps manage the flow of information, helps siphon off emotional distractions, and helps clarify, but he expects his technical people to be accountable for a decision. And sometimes Matt turns a decision over to his group because—no matter what he decided—*any* decision on his part would be viewed as favoritism. Making office assignments at the company's old location, for example, really had Matt in a tight spot.

Several years ago Matt's division was assigned space in a newly rennovated building. At that time, Matt's staff consisted of four specialists and a secretary/receptionist. Unfortunately, four offices were separated only by partial partitions. Two were "real" offices; Matt assigned himself one of these. Then he looked for some basis, such as seniority, for assigning the other. Everyone considered it a prize. Several criteria would *eliminate* one person or another, but Matt could find no objective characteristic that set any one specialist apart. Since the space was newly rennovated, Matt didn't dare ask for walls to be added or knocked down. He could, however, rearrange the movable partitions.

As with the consulting approach, Matt:

1. Checked everyone's understanding of the problem.
2. Clarified each person's role in making the decision.
3. Worked with the group to develop criteria for a good solution.
4. Encouraged data and idea sharing. Since Matt dealt with the whole group at one time, he was able to get good results with group-sharing techniques, such as brainstorming.
5. Summarized each person's ideas to his or her satisfaction. Matt saw to it that each person had, at a minimum, the satisfaction of knowing that he or she had been heard and understood *before* any decision was made.

But this time the group completed step 6: the group evaluated the decision. During that group evaluation, Matt observed each person, asked questions to encourage reluctant participants, summarized "where the group is" when it got stuck, and restated the original problem when the group got too far off track.

The group also completed step 7: the group made the decision. Afterward, Matt summarized what he understood features of the decision to be. When he was satisfied that everyone had the same understanding of the decision, he resumed administrative responsibility for seeing that it was carried out.

CONCLUSION

Pulling a team together isn't easy. No one can do it overnight. And it won't happen without setbacks and disappoint-

Flexible Management

Technical managers can build team cooperation by following the guidelines for *flexible* (not *formula*) management:

1. Notice how each employee works best: when each works best on a task with close direction; when each works best with little direction on the task, but with support in coordinating teamwork
2. Distinguish between tasks that require close direction and those that do not
3. Identify organizational conditions that require close direction and those that do not
4. Be familiar with several interaction models that can be adapted to suit their own personalities and a given situation

ments. But the effort to build team cooperation "justified itself . . . as a means of overcoming the limitations restricting what individuals can do" (Barnard, 1938, p. 230). In other words, the whole—the team—will become greater than the sum of its parts.

chapter seven

How Can I Cultivate Group Effort?

INTRODUCTION

Matt's work didn't end when he brought his team together. He still needs to foster group effort and to prevent polarization. How?

For one thing, Matt proceeds systematically. He takes the time to know his people individually, he complements the skills provided effectively by his group, he provides feedback, and he rewards group effort.

For another thing, Matt tries to avert polarization when a problem does develop. He encourages employees to talk about it, he gives employees feedback about the effects of the problem, he enlists the help of his people to remove barriers that block group effort, and he asks his people to try new patterns of behavior.

PROCEED SYSTEMATICALLY

Of course, no manager can "make" people work together. But good managers, such as Matt, have usually done a lot to

Building Team Cooperation

To foster team effort, technical managers can systematically try to:

1. Know employees individually
2. Complement group skills
3. Provide feedback
4. Reward group effort

make working together possible—even probable. Matt used some of these cultivation methods instinctively. Others he read about, tried out, and refined to suit himself and his people.

Know Employees Individually

This first method is an old standby. A recent study compared executives who made it to the top with executives who were derailed along the way and concluded: "Ability—or—inability to understand other people's perspectives was the most glaring difference between the arrivers and the derailed. Only 25 percent of the derailed were described as having special ability with people; among arrivers, the figure was 75 percent" (McCall & Lombardo, 1983, p. 31). Don't miss the happy inference that "to understand other people's perspectives" will do more than improve the odds for success on a lone project: it will also improve the long-term odds for success in an organization.

To understand another's perspective is to really *know* that person. Where does Matt start? By *listening* attentively and by *observing* attentively as he works and interacts with others.

How can you listen attentively?

First, put your own stream of thought on "hold." You're most likely to succeed at this if you look your employee straight in the eye while she talks, and "square away" with her physically. To square away, try to arrange yourself so that your eyes are at the same height as your employee's (easier to do if you're both sitting down). And sit like the Lincoln monument—but with more animation, of course. Keep your feet flat on the floor. (Notice how your body turns away from your employee if your legs are crossed.) And let your arms rest comfortably at your side or in your lap. (Crossed arms can seem like a barrier and "fidgeting" can distract both you and your employee.)

Now concentrate on what your employee is saying as if you would have to repeat it verbatim when she's through. Temporarily suspend judgment—don't rehearse the sage advice or the comforting anecdote that you might share later. Just listen.

Next, just keep quiet for a few seconds. Don't respond at all until you've counted silently to 5 or 10. Give your employee the chance to add a "footnote" without feeling pushed, and give yourself a chance for what she's said to sink in before you speak.

Finally, summarize what your employee has said in your own words but to her satisfaction. At this point it may seem natural to throw in some input of your own: advice, instruction, criticism, or reassurance. But each of these is likely to block further communication; each of these is likely to signal the end of the exchange to your employee.

For example, when Shelley virtually exploded about the "shaky" data base for some decision:

Matt squared away, he concentrated on what she was saying, he let what she said "sink in." Then he summarized what she said in a few of his own words: "You think we're moving too far too fast without double-checking our information."

He didn't cut her short or make light of what she said with a remark, such as "Well, time waits for no man—or woman! We've got to do something. I'm not afraid of a few risks!"

To observe attentively:

Notice patterns in your employees' behavior and in their appearance. Who's a morning person? Does anyone actually perk up after lunch? Who likes to work alone? Who would rather get other opinions? Who's always neat as a pin? Who looks like he combs his hair with an eggbeater? Who takes her lunch hour early? Who's taking a coffee break when?

Make it easy for each employee to come in contact with you during some part of his or her daily routine. That may be a snap for those of you who have five or fewer people to supervise—not so easy for those of you who have 10 or more. You can greet some by name as they arrive at work. Say hello to others at coffee break. Walk by workstations or step into offices at other times of day. Wish others a good evening as they leave.

Notice changes in individual behavior or appearance. If the change seems to be a positive one, reinforce it. When Stan (who usually looks like he combs his hair with an eggbeater) comes in "all spruced up," let him know that he really looks "sharp" (or whatever the "in" word is at the time). That's *not* the same as saying acidly, "Whose funeral are you going to, eh?" If the change seems to be a negative one, be sure the employee has easy access to you in case he or she needs to talk. For example, if Joyce (who usually looks like she stepped right out of *Vogue*) comes in looking bedraggled several days running without approaching Matt for a talk, he approaches her. He says something low-keyed, such as "I get the feeling that you're having a rough week." Then he's silent for the count of 10. If she shows no sign of opening up, he leaves her with a comment like, "Well, I just want you to know if you'd like to talk about anything, I'll be in all afternoon."

Complement Group Skills

To pull together instead of falling apart, members of a group must pool two kinds of skills: task skills (that move the task toward completion) and maintenance skills (that pull individuals together into a team). If any of the necessary skills are missing, it's up to the supervisor to supply them.

Task skills include initiating, seeking information, seeking opinion, giving information, giving opinion, elaborating, coordinating, and summarizing (University Associates, 1976, p. 136). Maintenance skills (or functions) include encouraging, gatekeeping, setting standards, and following and expressing group feeling (p. 137). And some skills contribute to both task achievement and maintenance of the group: evaluating, diagnosing, testing for consensus, mediating, and relieving tension (p. 137).

The better you know an employee, the better prepared you are to draw on his or her strengths. When a group shows high energy, for example, but has trouble getting the project moving, Matt might encourage Shelley (a superior organizer) to help get group activities coordinated. Later if that same group has made great progress on the task but is bogged down with infighting, he can enlist the aid of Larry, a really good "people person." He knows that Larry can help get pent-up feelings expressed openly and constructively. Larry can help the group get back on track by summarizing the progress that's been made and the work that's left to do.

The better you know your employees, the better you can fill in the gaps with role behaviors that are missing. If project members have interpreted group decisions differently several times, it may be up to you to test for consensus and understanding before a staff meeting adjourns.

Your knowledge of group roles combined with your knowledge of your people can also have some teriffic fringe benefits.

You don't have to be all things to all people yourself; you can draw on the strengths of your staff to move the project along and to pull your team together.

You can identify specific skills to develop in your staff to give them *and* you more flexibility.

You can develop a picture of the specific skills you want in a new hire when you have a position to fill.

Provide Feedback

A recent review of the Hawthorne studies suggests that the improved performance of workers involved resulted not from some mysterious "effect" but from the workers' improved knowledge of results—feedback (Parsons, 1974, p. 930). And another review of management studies concludes that feedback is "the action lever with the single greatest impact on productivity" (Cummings, Molloy, & Glen, 1975, p. 58). (An "action lever" is some characteristic of an organization that can be changed with the reasonable expectation of some desired result.)

Yet, let's face it: most supervisors continue to pile heaps of *evaluation* on employees (praise or blame) while serving up only very sparse portions of *feedback*. What's the difference? Well, by definition, good feedback is:

Specific
Measurable
Goal related
Visual when possible
Immediate

To hear "Well done!" may be rewarding for an employee. But it doesn't provide the same knowledge of results as "Your sales this month were up 10 percent from last month. That puts you within $10,000 of your quota for the year. And—as you can see by this chart—it puts the division within $30,000 of its goal for the year."

On the other hand, to hear "You really blew that one!" is only punishing to an employee. It gives the employees no real information that he or she can use to improve performance. But the employee could learn something from: "Acme could have benefited from all five features of our new model X. But in your sales presentation you mentioned only two. A review of this checklist before your next presentation might help you keep all five features in mind and as a result help you meet your quota for the month."

How about that annual performance appraisal, isn't that enough? Definitely not. In the first place, performance appraisals are usually too general to give an employee concrete information about how to improve. In the second place, helpful feedback doesn't come a year later. It comes right away: right after a sales presentation, in time to make a difference in the very next presentation. Furthermore, appraisals based on peer comparisons can actually be hazardous to performance: any system that "grades on the curve" as some of our college professors used to do is likely to produce "widespread discouragement, cynicism, and alienation" (Thompson & Dalton, 1970, p. 157).

Reward Group Effort

As his staff works on a project, Matt is sure to reward team effort as well as progress toward completion of the task. How? Well, first he pinpoints the behavior he's rewarding: "the way you and Larry pooled information"; "the encouragement you each gave after yesterday's setback." Then he provides some reward that his staff is sure to experience as rewarding. Remember that old saying, "different strokes for different folks." (See how often we come back to our original suggestion that you know your employees?)

In case you see dollar marks when we use the word "reward," take heart from this response in a survey of employees: "I now have found an employer who believes in me. I feel like a human being again instead of an android. . . . I have been handed responsibility without experience and performed superbly . . . just because someone up there had faith in me" (Renwick & Lawler, 1978, p. 56).

Nonmonetary rewards can come from social interaction, status, job environment, or job content. Here's an extensive list developed by supervisors and lead performers in a workshop on job instruction.

Social

Certificates of award

Letter to superiors/copy to employee

Letter to personnel file/copy to employee

Parties, showers, picnics, cookouts, and so forth

Award pins
Recognition for good job
Verbal praise, pats on back, "atta-boys"
Attention to person
Passing on compliments
Asking about family, interests, and so forth

Status

Title
Name on desk, door
Furniture
Private/more private office
Status symbols
Business cards
Name and recognition in newsletters
Access to special places

Job Environment

New equipment
Adequate air conditioning and heating
Ventilation
Less noise
Piped-in music
Private or semiprivate offices
Communication system
Adequate working space
Enough supplies
Less crowding
Office arranged to facilitate doing job

Job Content

Flextime
Choice of assignment
Schedule own work
Set own breaks and lunch
Higher-level responsibility
Assignment to special groups and task forces
More access to information
More training
Chance for varied assignments
Chance to specialize
Adequate electrical and office support
Opportunity to help set goals
Having resources readily available
Compliments on work
Sending up their reports to higher management
Change growth on job
Chance to get more experience

What about a group crisis? What special action is called for? Again, let's use Matt's technocrats as an example.

PREVENT POLARIZATION

Even the best "preventive" managers find themselves in the center of a crisis sooner or later. Those who can stand the heat while keeping a cool head themselves make it possible for a team to emerge from the crisis stronger than it was when

Preventing Polarization

To prevent polarization, technical managers can:

1. Name the problem and encourage people to talk about it
2. Give employees feedback about the effects of the problem on the group's work
3. Get employees' help to remove blocks to group effort and to try new patterns of behavior

it became *submerged* in it. Making it *possible* doesn't make it so, of course. But three steps to prevent polarization give managers their best chance (see box).

Name the Problem and Encourage Employees to Talk about It

Apparently John underestimated construction costs on his first project. That's not surprising for someone just out of school. Based on John's low estimate of cost, the company was awarded a contract. Now it's going to be really difficult to maintain quality without losing money on the job. Matt believes that it's possible, but really difficult to manage.

Yesterday, Matt held a group meeting in an attempt to tap the brain power of the entire group. It was a disaster. Shelley exploded at John. John retorted with a sexist remark. Roger (the budget specialist)—whose input would have been so valuable—closed up like a clam. How does Matt handle crisis situations like this one?

First, he names the problem and encourages his employees to talk about it. It may seem like a contradiction to say that the first step of a solution is to "name the problem." But when you have listened attentively, observed attentively, and pinpointed a problem, simply naming it—acknowledging it—can clear the air and make room for a solution. Like people, most problems have a first name and a last name: the first name is the feeling that has resulted, the last name is the reason behind the feeling. Bob Carkhuff suggests this formula for giving a problem it's full name: "You feel . . . because. . . ." (Carkhuff, 1972, p. 76)

Matt, for example, named the group's feeling this way: "You feel like giving up now because it just seems humanly impossible to meet the deadline with all the conflict we've been having around here."

It's a good idea to try the name out on a trusted friend before you share it with the group. You want to be sure it's:

Not judgmental

Not emotionally loaded

Matt would *not* give the problem this name: "You feel like copping out because of all the ridiculous scraps you've been having with each other lately."

It's probably a good idea at first to name the problem to one employee at a time. Otherwise, they may compete with each other for the chance to respond first or loudest and you'll have a skirmish on your hands.

After he named the problem, Matt encouraged each employee to talk to him about it. How? First, he just kept quiet for a few seconds. He counted silently to 10 or 15 and gave the employees a chance to speak up. When no one offered a reaction, he asked a few open-ended questions and allowed some time for them to respond after each one. His questions might include:

"What should we talk about to clear the way for a solution?"

"What do you think has gone wrong?"

"How do you see the problem?"

Before he left the group, he introduced some questions that suggest a solution, such as:

> "What do you think we should do next?"
>
> "How would things be different around here if they were just the way you wanted?"
>
> "What do you think we can do to get this project done on time and under cost?"

If his employees share their feelings and opinions, Matt is much better prepared to work with them on a solution. If employees offer neither feelings nor opinions, Matt lets them know that he's open to their input within the limits imposed by the situation. He might say:

> If anything comes to mind, I'd surely like to have your input. But Beyers insists on having my answer at lunch tomorrow. So I'll have to decide one way or the other by 10:30 A.M.—in time to document my reasons for it.

Give Employees Feedback about the Effects of the Problem on the Group's Work

Next, Matt gives employees feedback about the effects of the problem on work. As with feedback for "routine maintenance," he provides feedback that's specific, measurable, goal related, visual when possible, and immediate.

In a situation that's likely to be emotionally loaded, it's *especially* important that feedback *measure* the problem rather than *evaluate* it. This example sounds whimsical, but it clearly illustrates the difference.

Evaluation	Measurement
His ears look like an elephant's.	His ears are four inches across.

Here's an example suited to that office crisis:

Evaluation	Measurement
That outburst during the meeting yesterday was a fiasco.	The disagreement at yesterday's meeting cost us about 20 minutes. As a result, we couldn't get those plans in the five o'clock mail as we promised.

Even during a crisis, *something* may go well. And Matt is sure to notice it with feedback like the following: "Even with all the confusion here yesterday, you remembered to give Beyers the status report we promised him."

Get Employees' Help to Remove Barriers That Block Group Effort and to Try New Patterns of Behavior

When Matt feels that he has pretty good information about what's going on and how it's affecting the work, he reviews what he knows to answer these questions:

1. How are employees punished for making a group effort?

2. How are employees "locked in" to nonproductive behaviors?"

Most of us could name at least a few conditions that block the group effort we want. Perhaps some people feel punished because group meetings typically run past closing time and make them late for a carpool or for dinner. Perhaps group meetings often degenerate into a "lemon squeeze," where people sound off about the things they don't like without suggesting any constructive alternatives. Maybe one person receives disproportionate praise when a project goes well and others feel neglected. Or maybe a few people receive disproportionate blame when something goes wrong and they'd rather not get involved.

Most of us can identify a few instances of counterproductive behavior by an employee who doesn't know that he can choose to do differently. Perhaps John backs off from suggestions because he thinks it's a sign of weakness to accept help. And maybe Roger holds back important information because his last boss chewed him out whenever he reported bad news.

When Matt uncovers these problems within a problem, he uses the same approach he used before:

He names the problem and encourages employees to talk about it.

He gives employees feedback about the effects of the problem on work.

Then he enlists their help in removing the blocks he identified. He may need to:

Reschedule meetings so that they don't cut into personal time. Or get a consensus on time limits and then stick with them.

Develop some guidelines with the group for turning a "lemon squeeze" into a problem-solving session.

Use a checklist to be sure that he gives feedback to all employees who contributed to a successful project.

Be sure that his own approach to a problem is oriented toward finding a solution, not toward placing blame.

Model the behavior that he'd like John to choose: solicit his ideas and be sure he knows how they are used.

Invite Roger to share information when he thinks that Roger's holding back. And be sure to reward the sharing whether the news is good or bad.

CONCLUSION

Cultivating group effort requires a long-term commitment. No manager can "make" people work together. But successful technical managers systematically do those things that make working together possible—even probable.

And even the best "preventive" managers may find themselves in the center of a crisis. The technical manager who keeps a cool head has the best chance of preventing polarization when that happens.

Building Team Cooperation

To foster team effort, technical managers can systematically try to:

1. Know employees individually
2. Complement group skills
3. Provide feedback
4. Reward group effort

Preventing Polarization

To prevent polarization, technical managers can:

1. Name the problem and encourage people to talk about it
2. Give employees feedback about the effects of the problem on the group's work
3. Get employees' help to remove blocks to group effort and to try new patterns of behavior

chapter eight

How Can I Motivate Technical and Professional People?

INTRODUCTION

As we will discuss in other chapters, it sometimes bothers technical and professional people when they find themselves talking about more people-oriented subjects, such as motivation. We have to understand, though, that not everybody is completely devoted to and interested in doing a good job. Not everybody will carry out the job without hearing from the boss how well it's going and how it could be done better. We know some things about providing an environment that will motivate people to do their job, and there are some specific things we know about people that will help us in the whole concept of motivation. We talk about some of those things in this chapter.

To begin with, let's notice Al Bartow, who is the supervisor of the design section of Bill Morris's engineering group. Al has a number of people working for him, including three engineers, James Fox, Diane Wilson, and Thad McGee. As the conversation opens, we see that Al Bartow is discussing his people with Bill Morris, the engineering manager. They've been talking about the performance of the various people, and Al has raised a question.

Al: I sometimes wonder if I'm the right person to be a supervisor. My people have a lot of talent, yet I wonder if I'm making the best use of it.

Bill: You certainly have the talent, and it seems to me that they're producing pretty good work. What's the problem?

Al: Well, I don't know that it's a problem. It's just that these people are so different that it doesn't seem to me that any particular style of managing works.

Bill: Can you give me an example?

Al: Well, let's talk in particular about the three people who are doing the design engineering. Jim Fox is a very good engineer. He's thorough and he's precise, but at the same time, he's sort of touchy, very private, and seemingly jealous of any information he has. It's not unusual for him to find out some information and not tell other people about it unless they ask.

Bill: That doesn't sound very much like a good cooperative spirit.

Al: Well, that's not exactly true. He will tell them if they ask about it, but it seems that he likes knowing something that other people don't know.

Bill: Well, I think that's typical of a lot of engineers. There's a certain amount of power, as they say, in knowledge, and when engineers know something or get some information, they tend to store it up. Perhaps that's not unusual. Who else?

Al: Well, I have Diane Wilson. There's no doubt that Diane is the most intelligent engineer I have; she's probably one of the most intelligent people working in the entire organization. But she tends to be aloof with the rest of the people, and she's very pushy. If she has a design that she thinks is right, she's very insistent about it, whether it's with me, one of the other engineers, or somebody in another group. It's very difficult to talk to her if she thinks you're going to change something that she's done.

Bill: Does she think she's better than everybody else?

Al: I'm not sure that's right. She does tend to keep herself separate or aloof from the rest of the people, and they think she's stuck up or feels better than they are. But I suspect that a lot of the time she just travels in her own world. She's so good at concentration that you can walk up to her and start talking and she won't even hear you. It takes a while before she realizes that somebody is talking to her, and that doesn't always come across well with people who already think she's trying to be stuck up.

Bill: That's pretty typical of people who have good minds and who concentrate well. What about her pushiness? Is it a problem?

Al: Well, it's a problem in the sense that she sometimes rubs some people wrong because she comes across with some pretty strong assurance that she's right. She usually has backup data to prove her point, but in the field of design there sometimes has to be room for opinions.

Bill: What about Thad?

Al: Well, Thad has probably the best engineering background of anybody I have. He was born to be an engineer. His father was an engineer, and he's got a couple of brothers and a sister who are also engineers. The family doesn't know much of anything else. Thad is outgoing and I would say he's quite satisfactory. However, though he's the finest design engineer I've ever had, I'm not sure that he works up to his potential. But he never gives me any problems. He's very cooperative and helpful in areas where I need somebody to do some work that nobody else wants to do, and he thinks like an engineer.

Bill: Whatever that means.

Al: Yeah, I guess I'm not sure what that means either, other than he does his research and he understands that there are requirements for filling out forms and doing specifications. Those things just seem to come naturally to him. He doesn't complain about the paperwork; and if he has to change something, he doesn't complain about that either. He's interested in things other than engineering; he has a number of different hobbies and is one people call on when there's any kind of social affair. If they need someone to play the guitar or to sing, Thad's good at that and he likes to do it.

Bill: Well, it seems to me that you've got some good people. I think a lot of supervisors would be glad to have that kind of talent. How are they giving you a problem?

Al: Well, as I said in the beginning, I'm not sure that it's a problem. It may well be that I'm the problem. I just find that my style of supervision doesn't seem to work for all three of the cases.

Bill: Well, maybe you need to change your style.

Al: Well, maybe so, but I'm not sure that any one style would work with all three of them.

Bill: Don't look now, Al, but I think you have started to solve your problem.

Al: How's that?

Bill: We are going to have a hard time supervising if we have only one style of leadership to apply to all the different kinds of people. You need to take a look at each of these and maybe the other people that you have, too. Understand a little bit about their needs, what motivates them, what satisfies them, what bothers them, and supervise them accordingly.

UNDERSTANDING PEOPLE

Al has just learned some things that are important to him. We will deal with his specific problems a little bit later, but right now let's notice some things that we know for sure about people and see how we can use them in solving his problems. While three of Al's people have different personalities and obviously are going to be motivated by different things, we have to understand that there are many other people that have yet different personalities. Lest we get the idea, however, that it's a hopeless situation because everybody is different, let's notice that there are some things that people have in common and concentrate on those things. First, let's understand there are some things that don't motivate people.

We sometimes ride down the road and see a sign that tells us that a certain group of employees are unhappy enough that they have walked off the job. We usually see them carrying signs that ask for more money or better working conditions. If we've learned nothing else about motivation, we have learned that we will never pay people enough money to keep them motivated on a permanent basis. It's doubtful that we could stop and explain that to those workers so that they'd all pack up and go back inside. But we are saying that making more money in a situation that doesn't allow for people to use initiative, to get recognition, or to see that they have achieved something really won't motivate them very long. The same thing is true for improving the working conditions. One of the reasons that people notice the bad working conditions is that they lack motivation; they don't feel they have responsibility or they're working in a boring job. The truer this is, the more likely they are to notice the heat or the dirt or the noise, or be concerned about the color of the paint, the design in the rug, or the location of the parking places.

Having noticed some of the things that *do not* motivate people, let's go back and notice some of the things that *do* cause people to be more interested in doing their job and to be more committed to getting the job done. We've already mentioned several. For example, achievement is one of the main areas in which we can motivate people. Achievement is simply a matter of letting people know that they have accomplished something. For the whole engineering group we might put up a chart or graph showing the number of jobs we have done or the number of elements we have completed. This will give the whole team a look at how well they're doing. On the other hand, just finishing a task and being able to stand back and look at it is often achievement enough. People don't mind working if they can see some accomplishment, and they are much less likely to object even to hard work if there is a goal or an end to the task and if they can know that it was their effort that completed this task.

The second thing we want to talk about is recognition. We all want to be good at what we do, and we like to be better than other people at something. When we watch two children in the sand pile playing and listen in on their conversation,

Providing Long-Term Motivation

The following don't provide long-term motivation:

1. More money
2. Improved working conditions

we'll find that even five-year-olds want to be better, to have more than somebody else, or to do something that somebody else can't do. We'll hear them saying things like, "My truck is better than your truck," or "My car is faster than your car," or "My daddy can beat up your daddy." This doesn't really change as people grow up. If we listen to people as they travel to and from work or stand around during the work break or at lunchtime, we still hear them talking about the biggest fish, or the longest trip, or the worst employee. All of these things are efforts to get some kind of status or recognition, and the supervisors who recognize this need can use it as a means of motivating employees. They can point out to people that they've done a good job; they can give them a pat on the back; if it's a big accomplishment, they can give them recognition in the form of a letter or a banquet. The main thing is to let them know that they're doing something well and that you know they're doing it well. Most often this is most effective if we do it in front of other workers, but many times we need to do no more than just go by somebody and say, "Hey, I like the way you did that; that looks good."

The research that has been done over the years has suggested that the most lasting motivation we can get is the kind that comes from the very job itself. If the job is perceived by the employee as mundane, insignificant, or only part of a much bigger task, there's not going to be much motivation for very long. On the other hand, if employees know that this job is critical and that the organization is looking to them to perform well and that there is some significance in the end product as far as the overall operation is concerned, they're going to be more motivated.

Notice that we're saying that the perception of the job is important. The key point we have to make to technical supervisors is that much of the motivation available will come about as a result of people's perception of the job. For example, if someone comes in and wants some information and I simply turn around to one of my employees and tell him or her to get the information and give it to the person, that employee perceives that it's not a very responsible job. I sent that message to both the employee and to the person asking for the information. On the other hand, if I say, "You'll need to see Rod; he can get that information for you because that's what he does." It's the same job, the same assignment, and the same person looking for the same information, but I have changed the perception of the job. The perception now is that here's a person that knows what his job is and has a specific responsibility within that job, and that I have the confidence and the expectation that he will do his job. I'm sending a message to the person who came in that there's someone in charge of that particular thing, someone responsible for it; hence it's a more motivating job.

One of the problems that we've had in this whole area of looking at the job has to do with the advancements in technologies. There was time when one person did all the work. The cobbler probably made the whole shoe. But now the work is broken into such small parts that one person may cut out the leather, another may stamp the mold, another may put in the eyelets for the laces, another may do the sewing, and another may put on the heel; or the whole thing may be done by automation and nobody touches it at all. No one can say that he or she has the responsibility for making shoes, even if he or she works in a shoe factory. That's true for our own jobs. Even in

Providing Long-Term Motivation

The following do provide long-term motivation:

1. Achievement
2. Recognition/status

extremely technical areas, we begin to break the jobs down into such small parts that no one person feels the responsibility for a completed project.

FILLING NEEDS

One of the things that makes supervising difficult is the fact that not only do people have different needs, but they also have different ways of getting those needs satisfied. For example, we talked about the need for recognition. To some people that may be simply a pat on the back from the supervisor, but another person may require a letter from the vice president of science and engineering. We talked about achievement. To one person it may be just the self-satisfaction of knowing that he or she has accomplished something, but another one may need to see that he or she has done a better job than the last person doing that job, finished it earlier, or had it more widely acclaimed. People do have needs, and it is up to the supervisor to try to find those needs and satisfy them. We have to be careful that we don't become amateur psychologists or get into a psychiatrist's role trying to understand all the reasons why people do all the things that they do.

In this day and age many of the needs that were once satisfied in the home with the family are no longer being met. This may be because there is a change in the family unit or in the makeup of a family. It may be because there is a greater diversity of the kinds of things that we do. Maybe it's because we live much busier lives and don't spend as much time in the home. Whatever the reason, we find it happening more and more. Some of the needs that used to be met in the home now have to be met outside the home. For example, people have a basic need to belong to some kind of a social unit. It used to be that the home could take care of those needs, but increasingly we are finding that they have to be met elsewhere.

It's very difficult for the supervisor to meet those needs, because belonging to something means that I am accepted as I am, and the supervisor cannot always accept people as they are. The supervisor may expect people to be on time to work every day and to perform up to a certain standard. The supervisor may require dress to be of a certain kind or work to be performed in a particular way, or behavior to conform to some policy or company regulation. It means that people are not always accepted just as they are when they come to work. One person may have a negative attitude, another may be quarrelsome, and still another may tend to put work off. This is usually not acceptable on the job. The supervisor must find ways of helping these people belong to the unit and still get the work done and get the conformity that is necessary in a work team. Of course, the ideal is a situation in which the supervisor can make a distinction between the person and the person's performance. It is similar to the way that we make a difference between a child's behavior and the child itself; we still care for the child even though we don't care for its behavior. We must learn to accept individuals as individuals while we make sure that their performance meets the standard.

When we are thinking in terms of rewards, we have to understand that everybody wants rewards for the job they've done, but different people will want different kinds of rewards. For one person the reward might be the opportunity to do a bigger and better assignment that carries more responsibility. For another the reward might be public acclamation of the good job that has been done. For another the reward might be a half day off in return for the hard work that was performed. Successful supervisors are those who can look at their people and begin to understand what needs they have and how those needs can best be met. The supervisor who

Providing Long-Term Motivation

The following provide long-term motivation:

3. Meaningful work assignments

4. Meeting personal needs

- **a.** Belonging to a group
- **b.** Feeling important

treats everybody the same, gives all the rewards in the same way, gives all the recognition in the same way, and treats all the employees' needs with the same kind of fulfillment is going to have a difficult time. It's hard to supervise when we don't have the flexibility and understanding of how to deal with the different people in different ways.

Now, let's go back and take a look at some of the problems Al Bartow is having with the various people he has working for him. Let's see how these people might be motivated based on their individual personalities. We'll take them one at a time.

James Fox

Remember that Al explained to Bill Morris that Jim is a very good engineer but that he is touchy and sometimes seemingly jealous of information which he has; he is a very private person. The key to this is that he's a very good engineer. If he were not a good engineer, we would deal primarily with his performance and do whatever we could to correct that. In this case, what we're really working with is the fact that he is not always motivated in the right kinds of ways to help out the team, and he sometimes gets his feelings hurt. How are we going to motivate Jim in a way that will meet some of the needs he has?

One thing we know is that people are more likely to repeat the things for which they are rewarded, so we need to give some recognition to Jim for doing some of the things we like. Because he is a private person, and perhaps a little touchy or sensitive, we should not make a big show and have a big fanfare about something he has done; but when he does something we want him to repeat, such as giving assistance to one of the other engineers or sharing some of the information he has, it's a very good time to give him a pat on the back, verbally or physically, and say something like; "It's really good when you help out the others in the group, Jim." We don't make a big scene out of it, and neither do we need to make a big scene because he is keeping some of the information to himself. When we see him sharing the information or giving it to other people, we simply let him know that kind of behavior is satisfying to us and very pleasing to watch. It not only rewards him, it also lets him know that he's getting some recognition through us, his boss, for the work he is doing.

We understand that we're not likely to change his overall personality, but we can change his behavior by rewarding the good things he does and ignoring and not giving him recognition for things that he does which do not satisfy us. Primarily we want to reward him for doing a good job. When we counsel with him, we might make a further definition of a good job by telling him that our expectations and standards include helping other people, sharing information with them, and working as a team. When it comes time for an appraisal session or a review of his performance, we might mention that. If it is not a very serious infraction, we might not even make a record of it as something that he has done wrong; but we can mention to him that we'd like to see him working more closely with the group or that we appreciate the way he is growing into a good team member.

Diane Wilson

Diane is the most intelligent of the group, but she also seems to be aloof and aggressive in trying to have her way. Again we find that she is a good engineer; and when she tries to have her way, it is because she feels that she can document her design with accurate data. We are not faulting her for the job she's doing, but we may be faulting her for seeming not to listen to an alternative suggestion and for pushing too hard to get an idea approved when there are others who think there's a better way. We've already given her some satisfaction by allowing her to do the job and have total responsibility for it. The fact that she's the one shows that the job itself is a completed task and that she had it from beginning to end. She feels proprietary interest in the job, and that's always good. She has commitment to the job, and we want that. But there are times when she might need other people's opinions. At these times we should encourage her to get and consider additional help or viewpoints. As far as motivation is concerned, we need to let her make the decision so that she sees she has achieved this working relationship, rather than feeling that she has done it simply because we ordered her to.

We could probably force her to listen to other people, get ideas from them, and maybe even use their opinions; but we would very quickly kill her motivation. On the other hand, if we present her with a problem that says, in essence, "There are some problems that are arising because not everyone feels they are getting a complete hearing when you are presenting information. I have a great deal of confidence in your solutions, and they're usually very valid. I wonder how we can transmit the message to other people that you have done a lot of research, and I wonder how willing you are to listen to some of their ideas." While this may get some resentment from Diane, and might also cause her to become defensive, we have given her a meaningful task because we have given her the problem and made it clear that we expect her to solve it because she has the ability. We can even make it an assignment in which she will work on the problem and report back to us on what she is going to try the next time she is going to sell an idea. We might give her some suggestions on ways of selling her idea. We might give her a brief course on successful steps in selling. We might let her know that if she's going to get people to accept her ideas, she's going to have to show that they have some value. She's also going to have to make others believe that they have had some input into the idea. We want to continue to give Diane some recognition, although she may not need it as much as other employees.

Diane is doing a good job as far as the job itself is concerned, but she is not doing very much to motivate other people who work around her. For this reason we want to motivate her to use her intelligence and share it with the rest of the group. One of the ways of doing this is to create a situation where there's a team project in which she must share a problem as well as a solution. We tell her ahead of time that we know she can do this and we're sure the project will be a worthwhile one. As she begins to work with someone else, we want to encourage her to use her creativity and imagination and tell her we know we can count on her to communicate her ideas and to listen to the ideas of others. This will extend her idea of her belonging because now she can no longer be aloof but is a part of a team that we have constructed. As always, we want to reinforce any positive actions and not necessarily recognize any of the negative aspects until some other time. We want to be sure to set the standards or the outcome we expect on this project; and as this team gets closer to it, we want to support their actions constantly in a positive way.

Thad McGee

Thad McGee is probably the more typical worker. He is average, has a good background, has a lot of commitment to engineering, and does things in typical engineering kinds of ways; but he is no fireball in his work habits. After having admitted that he is a satisfactory employee, we might begin to wonder how to motivate him in additional ways. We would like all our employees to be working up to their capacity, and that includes Thad. What kinds of needs does Thad have? He probably needs to be recognized as a good engineer. Since his whole family is involved in engineering, they must certainly talk about engineering and the various projects they have. We can encourage and motivate him to do good work by giving him some kind of a letter of recognition, signed by us if necessary, commenting on the good job he's done on a particular project. This is something tangible that he can show his family to let them know he is appreciated.

We also want to encourage his willingness to take on difficult assignments, or different assignments, or even assignments that others in the organization consider less than desirable. This is not necessarily a bad thing for him, because he is apparently motivated by the recognition he acquires from doing jobs that others don't want to do. He probably explains to his family and friends that he's doing something nobody else wanted to do, and that's good. There's a chance that we can give him some more recognition or some appreciation for doing a good job that others didn't want to do. However, that's not the only thing Thad's good for, and we don't want to take advantage of him because he will take the less desirable jobs. We would hope that if we gave them to them, both Jim Fox and Diane Wilson would take these assignments and do a good job of them.

We can probably get a better picture of Thad's performance by giving him a very routine assignment which requires a certain amount of challenge, initiative, and responsibility. We can give him recognition by letting it be his job and letting him know that he will defend that design before other people and that we'll look to him for supporting data. This kind of a challenge is a chance for him to achieve in a very satisfying way since he really likes the routine engineering assignments. It also gives him that sense of belonging and being a part of the team. He feels he's going to do something for you as well as to represent the group as he explains the project to the long-range planning people or the project management people.

In all the things that we have said about motivation, we must realize that some people are ready for challenge, some people are ready just for recognition, and some people are ready only to be a part of a team and will be satisfied with that. If the employees feel that they are not getting much recognition for the job they're doing, it will affect their motivation and they will be particularly unhappy or dissatisfied if they see somebody else getting recognition for the job they have done. For example, if Al Bartow takes the work of any of his people and does the presentation to the other groups himself, or if he goes to his boss and explains what's happening but fails to give recognition to the employees for the part they've done in the work, they're going to be a very unhappy group and their motivation will go down. If any one of the work group continues to get more recognition than anyone else, the whole group will suffer.

At the same time it's not much recognition if we give everybody the same recognition all the time. If you give everybody exactly the same size floor space, exactly the same kind of furniture, the same nameplate on their desk, the same kind of filing cabinet, and exactly the same picture over their desk, this will not be a sign of recognition. It may be just a very convenient way to identify the people. Just because they have a private space like everybody else or the same number of square feet that everyone else has, we shouldn't expect those things to give any individual recognition. It's a case where not having them would cause motivation to suffer, but having them probably won't help. Typically, we give recognition on an individual basis when there has been a satisfactory or above-average performance. We don't have to go around all day, every day, patting everybody on the back, nor do we have to give recognition for every single accomplishment. It is important, however, to notice that the idea of recognition, or reward, is always good because people rarely run out of their need for being recognized. This means that when a person finishes a challenging assignment, we can make mention of it in some way or give recognition for it. The next time another challenging assignment is complete, we can do the same thing. We certainly don't hurt the employee by giving the recognition, and there's a chance that we might encourage and motivate the employee.

CONCLUSION

We have seen that it is important for us to know our people well enough to use motivation techniques that work best for them. As is sometimes said, "different strokes for different folks." The truth is, that's a pretty good saying. Everybody needs certain kinds of strokes, and different people need different expressions of those strokes. We increase motivation by allowing employees to achieve, by giving them recognition or status that lets them know they belong in the organization, and by reinforcing the good things they've done. However, when we're dealing with technical and professional people, it is most important to note that they are used to working on very difficult assignments, are in the habit of having challenges, and most important, have a record of success. Whatever recognition or reward we give these people and whatever reinforcement we give them, we certainly want to make sure that it does not come out as though we're surprised that they completed the task. Every assignment we give, every comment we have about the assignment, and whatever reaction we have at the conclusion of the assignment ought to imply that we expect them to do a good job and to finish on time with a superior product. They do not need frequent small rewards because they are not used to failing and have a "stick-to-itiveness" that will see them through. However, they are still human beings, and all human beings like to be appreciated for the work they're doing. When we show that appreciation, we are creating an environment where motivation can take place.

Providing Long-Term Motivation

The following don't provide long-term motivation:

1. More money
2. Improved working conditions

Providing Long-Term Motivation

The following do provide long-term motivation:

1. Achievement
2. Recognition/status
3. Meaningful work assignments
4. Meeting personal needs
   a. Belonging to a group
   b. Feeling important

chapter nine

How Can I Delegate to Technical and Professional People?

INTRODUCTION

Carole: You remember I told you three weeks ago that this project was on a tight schedule. Now I see there's no way we can meet the deadline! I can't believe you've let it drift.

Jody: Hey, that's not fair! I haven't "let it drift." I've been working like crazy to get it out, and you ought to know that. Besides, I tried to tell you last week I was having trouble, and all you said was, "It's your project, not mine." Frankly, I've been lost for the last several days.

Carole: Well, it was your project. You're supposed either to know how to do it or to find out how. That's my style of delegation.

This little dialogue may sound familiar to many of us. It—or some thing like it—goes on all the time. The key phrase was Carole's last one, when she said, "That's my style of delegation." Just to prove that, let's listen in on another conversation between Carole and John Green, another of her subordinates in the quality assurance engineering group.

Carole: John, why do I have the feeling you aren't pushing too hard on the optics group's request for a look at the possible alternatives for the present line run? Didn't we agree on a completion date last week?

John: Yeah, but some other things have come up. That's about the millionth time that question has been asked, and I'm getting tired of going through all the paperwork just to tell them they need to try something else.

Carole: But, John, that's what you're supposed to do! Your job is to give them paperwork so that they can go to the next phase of their quality control program. If you know the job so well, why does it take you so long to do the job?

John: Oh, I don't know. It's so routine. Why don't you get someone else to do that kind of stuff?

Carole: Because it's your job, and I assigned it to you. When I gave it to you, I expected it to be done without my having to follow up on every little detail. You know that's the way I work.

Yes, Carole, we begin to see that *is* the way you work. For what it's worth, your delegation style looks and sounds a lot like that of many other supervisors, especially in the technical and professional fields. It's called by various names, such as "Throw them in over their heads so they'll learn to swim," or "If I have to do your job, why do they need both of us?" or

"You're being paid to do the whole job, not just some of it, while I do the rest," or "Haven't you ever heard of completed staff work?" Having said all of that, we hasten to say that Carole is not completely wrong. There may be people who work for her who can operate very well under her style of delegation and who are the type of employee who needs just exactly that approach. The problem lies not with her style so much as with the fact that she has no flexibility. Everybody gets the delegation in the same way, regardless of their motivation or competency or experience. A little later in this chapter, we'll come back and look at Carole's problem.

DELEGATION: GENERAL GUIDELINES

Part of the maintenance of any work team, technical or nontechnical, is the proper use of delegation. There are some basic rules, the first of which is to see that the work is done at the lowest level of competency in the organization. There are exceptions to this rule, of course, and we'll see some of them; but the idea is that there are not many ways to justify doing work at a higher level when there are people at lower levels with the skills or the potential to do the work. Perhaps it would be best to ask ourselves, "Why delegate anything?" Of all the reasons that might be given, the best and most simple answer to that question is, "Because it's been proven over and over again that this is the best way to get the job done effectively." We've already seen ample evidence that it's the main function of the supervisor to get the job done through other people. The *process* of doing that is generally called "delegation." But let's look at some specific reasons why delegation is usually the order of the day.

1. Delegation, if handled properly, is an excellent way to motivate people. (On the other hand, poor delegation is one of the worst ways to motivate people; we've just seen this in the cases of John and Jody.)

2. Delegation is an excellent way to develop people. (It can also teach people bad habits and attitudes that will last them throughout their careers.)
3. When everyone's job is clearly defined, properly delegated, and openly understood, it becomes a very strong tool to use in keeping a team together as a cohesive group. (If people don't know what they're doing, and the work is improperly delegated and poorly understood, it is very devisive and destructive to any team effort.)
4. When the right people are doing the right things at the right levels in the organization, life is smooth and pleasant, and the supervisor has time available to accomplish the often tedious goals of planning and personnel administration. (When the wrong people are doing the wrong things at the wrong levels in the organization, life is full of misery and time is nonexistent for anything but crisis management.)
5. If delegation is properly planned, it is one of the best processes we have for assessing employee potential. (If it is mishandled, delegation can give false signals and mislead us in all kinds of ways about what people can and cannot do.)
6. When a person is given a task that is solely his or hers to do and the competence and motivation are there to do the job, the work can be satisfying and rewarding and can give a great sense of achievement. (If it is not assigned carefully and poor communication exists, the task can easily be viewed as just another job which is all hard work.)

So, what have we seen? We see that there seems to be two sides to every "coin" of promise that we have listed, and so it

General Guidelines to Delegation

To delegate successfully, technical managers should:

1. Delegate to the lowest level of competency in the organization
2. Get the job done through others

is. Delegation can be a curse or a blessing. That being so, it behooves us to learn as much as possible about it. Let's see some of the reasons for the things we've said so far.

Delegation as Motivation

How can getting more work motivate a person in any way? There is ample evidence that when viewed properly by the worker or subordinate, work is the best motivator that we can find. When people are asked to describe the best job they've ever had, they rarely tell about the jobs where they made great quantities of money for doing nothing. In fact, those jobs tend to be the ones they describe as the *worst* jobs. Ultimately, people get satisfaction from doing a job, doing it well, doing it on their own, and getting reward and recognition from it. People who are excited about their work, who like to get up in the morning and go to the job, who find time passing rapidly, who may miss lunch or work overtime on their own are people who are being motivated by the job, the work itself, not by money or benefits. (The money and benefits may get them to the job in the first place, but it will rarely keep them there if the work is not challenging, satisfying, or somehow able to motivate them.) Also, people may get excited by a "good" boss, may follow a "good" leader just because of the person who is the boss; but the ultimate motivation must come from the job, not the boss. When the assignment is dull, routine, and unrewarding, we will follow a leader just so far.

Notice that the key is that this motivation comes when the work is "viewed properly" by the worker. It becomes a matter of perspective of viewpoint of the worker, not necessarily the nature of the actual work. If the workers ever decide that it's just another job or that more work is being piled on them, it becomes very dissatisfying. In fact, the same assignment can easily be viewed in opposite ways merely by how the work is delegated. If the supervisor says something to the effect, "For this job I need somebody who can make some decisions on his own," it will be viewed by many as a challenge instead of just an ordinary assignment. On the other hand, if the message comes across as, "Look, I'm giving this to you because I don't have time to do it. Let's get it out as quickly as possible, okay?" it may come across as an insignificant assignment that the boss wanted to get rid of and is dumping on the nearest sucker. There's not much motivation to be found in that approach.

Delegation to Develop People

Any time we delegate something, it should mean we're giving somebody some work that is not routinely theirs, but rather is something that normally we would be doing ourselves. Because it isn't usually theirs, the employees will have to be trained to handle this new assignment, hence the development aspect. But the training has to be good, pertinent, specific, and according to acceptable on-the-job training standards. With most people, the worst thing that we can do is just give them an assignment, maybe a deadline, with no help on the correct procedures for the job or the manner in which we will evaluate the finished product. In the event the employees do finish the assignment, there is a good chance that some things will be done incorrectly or that some of the approaches will be wrong. If we aren't able to correct these, we'll find that the employees may have learned some habits that will live with them for the whole term of their employment. The sad part is that they may be spending a lot of time from now on unlearning things that they learned just to get the first job done on time. Instead of it being a good learning and development exercise, both the employee and the organization will suffer consequences for a long time to come.

There are those who make a distinction between *training* and *development*. The difference is perhaps obvious in that training is immediate for a specific job at hand, whereas development is a long-range process which may include some training. If we use these definitions, when we talk in terms of successful delegation, we're really talking about development. When we delegate a task, the employees must be trained, but they will have long-range benefits from having developed a skill that will last them through subsequent times they perform that task. It will also serve as a basis for additional delegation (and training) in the future. Going back to motivation for a moment, it is important that the employees see that they've learned this new skill and that it will lead them into something other than just more unrewarding assignments. It is a sad thing to hear an employee say something like, "I don't see why I get saddled with this new assignment. I don't have time to do my *own* job, much less the *boss*'s job!" Again, it is often the employees' *perception* of the job rather than the job itself.

Defining the Job for Team Building

One interesting experiment that is occasionally done is to ask subordinates to define their jobs, giving the standards as they understand them, and ask them to make a statement about just what their bosses expect of them. With this information at hand, the bosses are then asked to give the same information about these same subordinates' jobs. As one might suspect, there is always a vast difference in the way the boss and the subordinates see things. When the results are mixed up and names removed, there is rarely a time when an outsider can match up the jobs as seen by the subordinates with the jobs as described by the bosses. Needless to say, this kind of arrangement isn't likely to do much team building! We're talking about delegation, so the point to be made here is that we're doing a poor job of delegation when we don't give the specific expectations, standards, and desired procedures along with the description of the work itself. If we've ever heard, "Oh, I didn't know you wanted it *that* way," we know that we have an employee who hasn't been given all the information needed.

The hazards are many in any kind of delegation, but if we expect to maintain a suitable team by using delegation, it is urgently necessary for us to be certain that we've properly laid out the work, the areas of responsibility, the expectations of each of the people working for us, and some reasonably

Reasons for Delegation

Technical managers should delegate so as to:

1. Motivate people
2. Develop people
3. Build teamwork
4. Provide supervisory time for other functions
5. Assess employee potential
6. Give a sense of achievement

clear delineations among the various assignments to different people. This is more than just writing job standards. It includes defining jobs as they are delegated. When we give an assignment to someone, we need to make certain that the person has an idea of what we expect, when we expect it, the form the finished product will take, the benchmarks along the way, and any training that will need to take place. Not all of the jobs we delegate will need that, and we won't give everybody the same kind of assistance, but *we* ought to know all those things in case there is a question that needs to be answered about any of them.

Operating at the Right Level

It is often said that authority tends to rise in the organization, while responsibility gets pushed down. If we fail to delegate properly, we may get the wrong things done at the wrong levels, causing all kinds of problems in the team effort. The idea of delegating is for the purpose of getting something done at a lower level because there is competency there. It makes no more sense to have a graduate engineer sweeping the floor than it does to have a supervisor adding up numbers on a report to check their accuracy. Part of the team maintenance process—as far as delegation is concerned—includes finding out what people can do at lower levels and giving them well-defined jobs in which to use that ability. Imagine a situation where the jobs are assigned, but with little definition as to exactly where the lines of responsibility are drawn—either vertically or horizontally. There are deadlines, but the various people aren't sure who has the authority to make which decisions. There is apparent overlap among the various activities; and as the deadlines approach, there is confusion and frustration all needlessly brought on by poor delegations of tasks. People begin to make excuses and place blame on others. Pretty soon the projects are late and there is so much dissension among the team participants that it's not even right to call it a "team." Sooner or later the individuals, not the supervisors, will be blamed for the problem. It will go on somebody's record as "not able to meet deadlines," or even worse, "not able to accept responsibility." Unfortunately, in these kinds of situations, the supervisors often go free, unscathed!

The idea of getting the work done at the proper level is seeing not only the work well defined, but also that everyone knows who has the authority to make what decisions. The amount of decision-making power that a person has, as well as the times it will be necessary to get higher approval, should be part of the original assignment. If there are others who can or need to approve of a particular thing, that should be pointed out, too. In any effort, all energies should be put toward getting the job done, not getting it approved or looking for someone to give that approval. When authority can be given along with an assignment, there should be no hesitation to do so if the project and the people warrant it.

Planning Delegation as Assessment Potential

What better tool can we find to see if a person has the ability to do a job than to have them doing all or some of that job? That's one of the great advantages of the delegation process. We delegate a task to someone, watch the person perform, evaluate the person's success or failure, and come away with a good view of the person's ability to handle something that he or she has never done before. It *is* a good tool, and it works. However, there are some drawbacks; mainly, it requires some good planning. It doesn't just happen. We can't just hand somebody an assignment on the spur of the moment, without much thought ahead of time, and expect a successful assessment process. We tend to think of delegating things to people without training them or discussing it ahead of time as a quick means of testing them. But what are we really testing? If someone asks us to go fly a jet plane without giving us any training or preparatory work, the outcome is pretty predictable. It doesn't mean we're a bad pilot, or that we could not learn to be a good one. It does mean that somebody is going to have to pay the price for a smashed-up plane and a dead pilot. So it is with the jobs that we delegate to people without letting them know we are looking at them to see how well they do, or that they can have training, help, or some recourse if along the way they find something they can't do.

As we will see in a little while, there are two elements that must be considered in delegation of tasks and in the procedures we use in carrying out that delegation. First, we have to consider the person's competence to do the job. That means that we must think about the person's past experience relative to this particular task, knowledge level with regard to that task and motivation. We have to look at things like the person's ability to work independently, willingness to put in the effort required to complete a task by the deadline, and the history of completing tasks by their deadlines. By looking at what has happened in the past (the history of motivation), we can see just how eager the person is to do a job. Second, we consider whether or not this is a motivating task within itself. If it is in fact something the employee has done for a long time, it's not really anything new; and he or she probably won't be all that motivated just to do another routine task. We must also consider whether or not there are a lot of other people working on this same project and whether or not there is a clear delineation between what this person does and what the others do on this same assignment.

Our goal is to improve a person's ability to contribute to the organization and to relieve ourselves so that we can do more important tasks and more planning for organizing so that we can make better use of our own time. If we have the right reason for selecting a task to delegate to someone, and if we choose the right person for the right job, we can be sure that we're going to do as well as can be expected in the delegation effort. Part of the skill is making sure that the person has the competence and the motivation. As we will see in a moment, if that's not the case, we still have some expectancy of success in the field of motivation.

FLEXIBILITY IN DELEGATION STYLE

If we go back to the beginning of this chapter and look at Carole's approach to delegation, we'll see that she was in fact making a number of mistakes. She was digging a hole for herself and was already beginning to slip into it. Her statement, "That's my style of delegation" shows that she had very little flexibility. We can also see that she violated some of the rules we just looked at. In both cases, although the people were different, she mismatched their motivation to their competence. For example, in the first case, Jody had a competency problem. She wasn't a bad employee, she just didn't know what she was doing all the time. She had neither the background nor the help from Carole to carry out her assignment. She said, "I tried to tell you last week that I was having trouble," and Carole answered, "It's your project, not mine." Jody needed some help, some guidance, and some information, but she got none of that from Carole.

On the other hand, John objected to dealing with something he had already done as he said, "millions of times," and by his own admission he just didn't have the interest or motivation to do the job. Carole did not provide the follow-up, the tracking, to see that the job got done. Her statement at that time was, "You know that's the way I work."

General Guidelines to Delegation

To delegate successfully, technical managers should:

3. Use flexible delegation styles

Many times supervisors will use Carole's style of delegation and as a result will get poor performance because different people need different styles. Let's look at a way that Carole could have done a better job of delegating to these two people, as well as other people. Imagine, as we see in this figure, that there are four kinds of people that we must deal with. Actually, all people fall in between these extremes, but let's talk about the extremes and see how they fit on the matrix we have in this illustration. The four different kinds of people are as follows:

High experience, low motivation
High experience, high motivation
Low experience, low motivation
Low experience, high motivation

Each of these four requires a different style of delegation. Let's look at each one of them to see where Carole's delegation problem fits.

High Experience, Low Motivation

When the employees have a great deal of experience or competence, we don't have to train the people to do the work or increase their experience level. We don't have to show them how the job had been done before, and we don't have to get them to talk with other people who have done the job. They know how to do it, and they have demonstrated that they can do it. They have the competence and the knowledge to carry them through. But because their motivation is low, we will have to do some tracking and some follow-up. We must set some deadlines and check to see if those deadlines are met. We are going to have to sell the project to these people by letting them see the importance of it. They will need to know that it is their assignment and that they're expected to get that assignment done on time. They need to know that we understand they have the competency to finish the task, but that we will be following up on their progress, watching to see that it meets the deadlines and that the various milestones and checkpoints are observed and on schedule. This is where Carole fell down in dealing with John. She knew that John knew how to do the job, and she couldn't understand why he took so long. She didn't recognize that it was his low interest or motivation, rather than a lack of skill or competency that was keeping him from doing it. Instead of hearing Carole say, "When I gave it to you, I expected it to be done without my having to follow up on every little detail," we really want to hear her say, "John, I gave you this job because you knew how to do it, and I certainly had every right to expect it to be done. On the next assignment we will set the deadlines and do some checking, and I'm sure you will get the job done on time."

For example, if John's next step is to call the optics group to see if they're still interested in the alternatives, Carole might say, "John, when we finish this discussion, why don't you call the optics group and then get back with me this afternoon to let me know what they say." This way Carole has set up a specific assignment with a deadline and a means of checking to see that it has been done. She did not leave it up to John to volunteer the information; she simply set up the appointment and expected him to be there with the information. In her discussion with him she said that they had agreed on a completion date. What she should have done is to agree on more than a completion date so that John would have to demonstrate that progress was being made toward completion. She might say something like, "Since the completion date is on Friday, why don't we set a time on Tuesday afternoon around 4:00 so that you can show me your progress and I can see if you're needing any help." She may even want to set up another follow-up date on Thursday morning or at some other time during the week. Then, when John begins to meet those deadlines, she will know that motivation has come up to the point where he is able to do the job without being checked. At that point, Carole will certainly want to back off and not push him so hard so that it doesn't look like she thinks he has no interest in doing the job. Thus, we see that there are some particular skills involved in dealing with people that have high experience or high competence and low motivation.

High Experience, High Motivation

This is perhaps the ideal because we're looking at someone who knows what they're doing and is interested in doing it. This is somebody who simply needs to know what it is we want and waits for us to get out of the way so that he or she can get started doing it. It's a good situation, and it's the ideal that every supervisor dreams of. Neither John nor Jody fits into this category. This is an employee that, in the past, has demonstrated enough skill and enough experience in the same type of assignment that we know we don't have to do any training or explain the step-by-step process needed to get the task done. We know we won't have to refer to the manual or put this employee with someone else in order for him or her to learn how to do the job. We also know that we won't have to dedicate a lot of our time to get the job done. Because the employee also has high motivation, it is not necessary for us to plan on doing a lot of tracking, follow-up, or checking to see what kind of progress is being made. All we have to do is let the employee know the standard of performance we're looking for and the deadlines we've set and let him or her go to work.

Even though this is the ideal situation, we need to remember that if this is something the employee has done many times before, it may seem like just a routine job which at some point may get boring. This means that to keep the employee interested in doing this kind of work, we ought to offer reinforcement—some reward, praise, or recognition to let the employee know that something has been achieved. Also, we ought to make ourselves available to let the employee know that he or she can count on us for help if it is needed. We don't want to put the employee in a bind by saying, "I know you won't need any help on this," or, "I know you can do this project by yourself," making it embarrassing to ask us for any help. We simply need to say, "This is the kind of thing that you have done well before, and I'm sure you know by this time that I'm available to help any time you want it. Let's don't let the project slow down because you run into a snag of some kind that you can't handle. Just call on me if you need any help; otherwise, I'm sure you will meet the deadline." Such a statement has all the necessary reinforcement and encouragement, but it also makes it easier for the employee to come to us when there's some help needed.

Low Experience, Low Motivation

It is very difficult to delegate to someone when he or she has neither the past experience and competence to do the job nor any particular interest or motivation in accomplishing the task. It's not very often that we find ourselves delegating to this kind of person, but yet there are some reasons why we might. For instance, we may simply be shorthanded and need some employees to pitch in and help. However, the employees may feel that it's not their job or that they have something else to do. They may be discouraged because it's not something that they are readily able to do. In fact, the low motivation may come because they don't know how to do it. On the other hand, they just may have other interests and would rather be doing some other part of the job. Whatever the case, it does happen; and we need to know the best delegation style to use in that situation.

By now we've seen that whenever there is low experience, training is important. If this is a person who has never demonstrated the ability to accomplish this task, we know we will have to give some guidance. There must be some coaching and assistance along the way. We don't dare turn this employee loose and say, "Just do the best you can." It wouldn't be fair to us or to the job, and it certainly wouldn't be fair to the employee. Because there is a lack of competence and experience we need to offer the employee as much encouragement and assurance as possible, letting him or her know that there will be training and assistance and that we will be helping. We need to let the employee realize that there is nothing wrong with not knowing how to do something that he or she has never had the experience or the opportunity to learn. We might also let the employee know that this is a good opportunity to expand his or her abilities, to become useful to the organization, and ultimately to derive personal benefit.

We have already seen that when there's low motivation, we have a selling job to do, as well as some tracking. The employee needs to know that this is an important assignment, that we have selected him or her over other people, and that we don't see it as a means of punishment because of poor past performance. We're asking the employee to do it because we need the job done and have selected him or her to do it. We should make it perfectly clear that this is an important task that will help the organization and that it needs to be delegated to someone who will get it done.

There are two reasons why we need to do some tracking. The employee not only lacks the motivation to work independently, complete the task by the deadlines, and to stick to the assignment, but also lacks experience. Since we are having to motivate and train the employee, we need to watch the performance as we follow up on the success of both our training and our motivation. This can be an excellent opportunity to change this employee's attitude toward the work, to improve his or her performance, and to provide us with an employee who in the future will be much more valuable to us.

Low Experience, High Motivation

When we look to the exchange that Carole had with Jody, we see that Jody really fits into the category of being motivated to do the job but frustrated because she doesn't know how. In the case of low experience and high motivation we have perhaps the most delicate situation. In delegating we have to be very careful when we're dealing with a person who wants very much to do the job and has shown by past efforts that he or she will do whatever it takes to complete the job, but who unfortunately is not competent enough to handle the assignment. If we use Carole's approach, we may kill the motivation. Carole just used her regular style and more or less left the project up to Jody to do or die, or sink or swim. There's an old adage which says that the best way to teach people to swim is to throw them in over their heads, but we should always remember that it's also the best way to drown somebody who can't swim. Jody wants very badly to do the job and to accomplish the task, but she's having trouble. She needs some answers, some help, and some training; she needs the advantage of someone else's experience. If we don't help her, frustration is going to cause her to become either a bitter or a disinterested employee. Not only will she not get the job done because she lacks training and experience, but she will also lose her motivation.

Since this situation involves someone who has very high motivation, we obviously don't have to do much of a selling job in order to get the employee motivated and don't have to do any tracking to make sure the job gets done. We don't have to set or follow up on deadlines to see that the employee is devoting energy to the task. We don't have to convince the employee that this job is significant to our operation and that it needs to be done well. All of this is wrapped up in the high motivation.

It is important, however, that we provide the opportunity for the employee to learn. The tracking we do is in the certain places we have mutually agreed need follow-up on the training to make sure that we've done a good job of showing the employee how to do the work. The employee needs to know that we are available to answer questions and that mistakes that will possibly be made can become a learning experience. It is important that the employee finishes up with a good feeling about the way things went, with the same motivation that was high to begin with and with more experience, hence more competence, to do that same task later.

Now let's notice the accompanying figure to see all of this put together. We see that when motivation is high and experience is low, we need training and follow-up. When experience is high and motivation is low, we need selling and tracking. When both are low, we have to do the training and the follow-up to be sure that the training is working, as well as continue to sell the need for the job and track the employee to see that he or she meets the deadlines. When both experience and motivation are high, we have to do very little of any of these. There is no need for motivation or tracking, and there's no

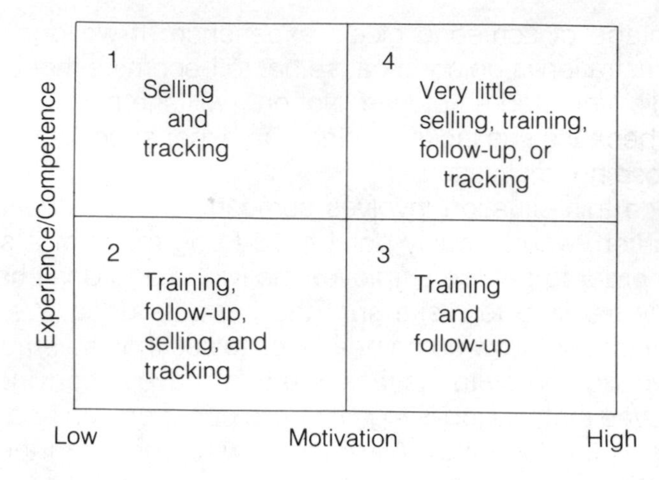

need to train or follow up, since the employee knows how to do the job and will most likely get it done.

Now, let's look again to see how Carole might treat these two employees in view of what we have seen so far, going back to the original assignment of the particular project instead of starting with their conversation with Carole. In the case of Jody, we have seen that she's in block three (high motivation but low competence or experience). This means that we are going to have to give her some training, follow up on that training, and let her know we are available to help. That pretty well defines what we are going to say to her. Notice the following discussion:

Carole: Jody, we've got a project here that I think would be a good learning experience for you. It's on a tight schedule, but I'm sure you can make it, because your enthusiasm in the past has made it possible for us to get some projects through.

Jody: Well, thank you. I appreciate the compliment, but I do like an opportunity to learn as much as I can. If you think I can help, I sure would like to try.

Carole: I appreciate the attitude you have always shown. Let me suggest that this project is one that you haven't worked on before, and we're going to work with you in the very beginning to let you see how to get started on it. I'm going to get some target dates for you; and as you go along, I want you to know that I am here to help you in any way I can. Since you haven't done it before, I think it's a good idea for me to suggest when you ought to have certain phases of it finished. If you get through it ahead of time, certainly you can go on to the next phase. However, if you see that you are in trouble, let me see what you are doing so I can help. In the future, of course, you can probably handle these projects on your own.

Jody: Sounds good to me; I know you are always available, and I appreciate your help, but I would like to do as much as I can on my own. I will check with you, though, if I have any problems. Then as you give me some training, I'll probably have some questions. I appreciate your interest in me.

We see that Carole has made it clear that there's going to be some training and some follow-up and also that she understands that Jody knows just exactly how fast she needs to be going and when the particular checkpoints will be. Therefore, Carole sets some deadlines for completing certain parts of it, giving Jody some freedom to operate within that time frame. Notice that she makes sure Jody understands that the checkpoints aren't just to see that she isn't goofing off or putting the assignment aside for something else, but rather they are simply a means of doing some follow-up training.

Now let's take a look at John Green, another one of the subordinates in the quality assurance engineer group that works with Carole. You remember that John feels that his assignment is not all that important because he has done it so many times and knows it so well. It's a case that falls in block one, which means that we must do something to let him know how important this job is and follow that with some tracking to make sure that he does it. Notice how Carole goes about this:

Carole: John, I've got a project here that I would like for you to work on. It has to do with the optics group's request for some possible alternatives for the present line running. They're working on the quality-of-work team that we talked about, and I'm not sure they have the best alternative.

John: Well, I've answered that question a million times for a lot of other people, and I'm sort of getting tired of going through all that paperwork just to tell them that they need to try something else.

Carole: I can surely appreciate that, but you understand that this particular group is working very hard to save us some money, find a better way of doing their job, and get the present run through. In the past, this group has done a pretty good job when they've gotten all the information, and we have some pretty good records on the amount of money they have saved us by their suggestions.

John: Yeah, I suppose that's so, but it seems to me that you ought to get somebody else to give them that information. I'm getting sort of tired of it myself.

Carole: The only problem with that, John, is you know more about this than anybody else; and if they are willing to spend their time and effort in trying to find a better way of doing it, we certainly want to follow up on that and give them the help that somebody like you can offer. I would rather have them talking to someone who has a lot of knowledge than someone just starting on the job. This way we can give them the answers quicker, and they can come back with some suggestions. Of course, you will need to be in on the end of it to see how good those suggestions really are; we would like your opinions at that time, too.

John: Well, I will admit there have been some pretty good suggestions turned in, and I do know something about it; but you don't have to badger me. I'll do the job if necessary.

Carole: I know you will, John. Here's what I would like to do. I'd like for you to call them this morning and see what questions they have, then check with me right after lunch to let me know what they said and how it came out. I want to keep up with it, too. Then let's take another look at it on Thursday morning to see how they're coming. Let me know the number of calls you get from the other people, too. I think it would be good for me to know what is happening. We'll set some time limits on this so we can be sure to keep up with it.

John: Well, most of the stuff is just routine, and I can handle it.

Carole: I know you can handle it—no problem with that, but I'd like to know it is going smoothly. If necessary I may need a meeting between you and some of us to see if we can slow down some of the calls we are getting and also to see if we can offer them some more help. I appreciate what you are doing and hope you will continue the good work.

Remember that John falls in block one of our chart. We recognize that he is high in competence and low in motivation, but that doesn't mean he is a bad employee. He's simply tired of doing the same thing and lacks motivation to give answers he has given to a lot of people a lot of times before. Carole's approach is one of selling him on the importance of what was being done and tracking him in the assignment. Notice that she points out that he is the best one for the job and knows more about it than anyone else. Considering that they are putting their own time into the matter trying to improve things for the organization, the least we can do is give the best help we can. The implication is that certainly John ought to be willing to do as much for the company as these people who are trying to improve the quality of the product and the production of that product. Notice, also, that while Carole does a good selling job and gives good reasons for doing the job and having John do it, she also has some good tracking techniques. She says, "Make a call this morning and let me know this afternoon what you found out," but she doesn't stop there. We then hear her say, "Let's get together Thursday with them." These are all efforts to track John without riding herd over him. He feels a little pressured when he says, "You don't have to get involved; I can handle it." She resists the temptation to back out by admitting that he doesn't need that much follow-up as far as the technical topics are concerned. She reminds him that she wants to be in on it in case there is something she can do to reduce the number of calls and requests that he is getting and to see what things are going smoothly.

John is a good employee, but because he lacks the motivation to do this particular assignment, the supervisor sees fit to do a selling job and also to provide the tracking. If this job is ever done properly and on time, it will require the supervisor to follow up, watch the progress, and check periodically to see that things are going properly.

CONCLUSION

The conclusion to this is simple enough. As we've already seen, people that are high in motivation need less follow-up and less tracking. If they are high in competency or experience, they need less training and follow-up. If they are low in motivation, there needs to be selling and tracking. If they are low in experience or competence, they need training and follow-up. The experienced supervisor knows that we don't use the same style of delegation for every employee. Before we assign a task, we do a mental calculation based on past experience to determine how well this person has done in meeting deadlines on similar assignments and what level of knowledge and experience he or she has on this kind of assignment. Then the supervisor makes the assignment in accordance with this information. Delegation is a tremendous way of developing employees; and most of the time, it's the best way to get the job done. If we follow the rule of having this work done at the lowest level of competency in the organization, we must become good at delegation. Technical and professional supervisors frequently are poor at delegation, mainly because they have spent so much time very close to the work and know so much about it, that they find it easier,

General Guidelines to Delegation

To delegate successfully, technical managers should:

1. Delegate to the lowest level of competency in the organization
2. Get the job done through others
3. Use flexible delegation styles

quicker and more satisfying to do it themselves. Since the best definition we can have of a supervisor is one who gets the job done through others, we must conclude that whenever the supervisor is doing something that should and could be done by people at a lower level, the supervisor is in fact, in those instances, not a supervisor, but a doer.

Reasons for Delegation

Technical managers should delegate so as to:

1. Motivate people
2. Develop people
3. Building teamwork
4. Provide supervisor time for other functions
5. Assess employee potential
6. Give a sense of achievement

chapter ten

How Should I Handle the Poor Performer?

INTRODUCTION

No matter what the group being supervised—technical, professional, older, younger, men, women, high or low skills—there will be those who do not perform up to the standards set and expected by the organizations. By definition these become "poor performers." When it happens in the high-tech area, it is often a more difficult problem to deal with, because the job-measuring processes are less accurate and the emotional and psychological impacts may be higher than with other types of employees. Nevertheless, supervisors must deal with and take steps that will produce acceptable performance on a consistent basis. There are some specific actions which, if taken, will make the job easier and more effective. We'll look at some of them and see how good supervisors have successfully handled similar problems.

REMOVING OBSTACLES TO GOOD PERFORMING

Most work places and work standards are fraught with contradictions and task interferences that actually can prevent doing the job properly. Many can be removed by the supervisor; some cannot. For example, there may be a push for completing quotas, getting out production, meeting deadlines, all of which give an air of urgency and time contraints, while another push is being made for safety and quality and a relatively serene work environment. Something as simple as this can create confusion and frustration among the employees and cause them to wonder which is really the top priority. It's not enough to say that "we want all those things." Without realizing it, the supervisors quickly give priorities by putting emphasis on specific things. When an employee is taking more time than the boss thinks necessary to get a report "just right" and the boss begins to ask urgent questions about completion dates, the message sent is that "getting it out" supersedes "getting it right."

Another frequently present obstacle is simply *poor supervision.* An untrained boss can do more to reduce satisfactory performance than can any other single action or activity present on the job. A supervisor who uses management styles incorrectly can alienate the work force, reduce the morale level, cause dissension, and even produce high absenteeism and turnover, without ever realizing the cause. The managerial skills given in Chapter 6 aren't just options; they are critical for success at dealing with people. They have a history of success. As we've said before, technical and professional people *tend* to resist the notion that something as intangible as "management style" has any place in their world. Frequently, they also find themselves untrained, hence have to "wing it" in doing their people's chores. Often the result is poor performing subordinates who get the blame for being unsatisfactory, while the supervisor gets off uncharged with any crime.

The solution to this problem isn't an easy one, but it is certainly a possible one. Careful examination of the tasks to see if, indeed, there is a conflict or cross-purpose in any of them will offer the quickest help in solving this part of the problem. Next, by looking at how priorities are set and what gets emphasized when there is a crisis, we can quickly tell if we've been realistic in setting our goals, standards, and priorities. Finally, if we seriously study material like that presented in this book and elsewhere, recognizing that there is a lot of research and validation behind it, then look at our supervisory efforts matched against these things, we'll know just how good a boss we really are.

PAVING THE WAY FOR GOOD PERFORMANCE

If we remove the things that present obstacles, we make it more possible for us to get better performances. But there is a positive side, too. There are some things that we can do to enhance the performances of our people. For example, there is no substitute for a good set of job standards or expectations. While the nature of the kind of work and the kinds of workers talked about in this book make it difficult to set some of the work standards in completely measurable and observable terms, it isn't an impossible task. If we sit back and view it in terms of all the difficulty that it presents, writing/ setting standards becomes a frustrating and very undesirable job. On the other hand, if we stop and think a moment about which of our employees are performing well and which are not doing so well, we quickly realize that we *do* have some kind of stan-

Removing Obstacles to Good Performance

To remove obstacles to good performance, technical managers should:

1. Set good job standards, approved by the organization
2. Identify acceptable, personal standards of the supervisor

dards or we wouldn't be able to answer the question of how well they're doing. It's dangerous to set standards by comparing employees, but at least that shows us how we are making decisions about standards. We simply ask ourselves, "Why do I think this person is doing better than that one?" The moment I can answer that question, I've shown I do.

Good supervisors recognize that it's not enough just to set standards for the actual work performance. Each supervisor has some personal standards that are peculiar to him or her. These are as much a part of the standards as any other standard, since we will be evaluating the employees on this standard or expectation. For example, the job may say that a proposal should be written a certain way, couched in certain formal language, and finished by a certain specific time. All of that makes up part of the job standard. At the same time, the supervisor may expect the employee to accept certain responsibilities, make certain decisions, and solve certain problems with regard to this proposal. The supervisor may expect the employees to make suggestions on ways of improving the proposals in the future or better ways of packaging the material. He or she may even expect the employees to make presentations about the proposal to other management levels. That is the supervisor's personal standards, and the employee will be evaluated on these as well as the job standards. As long as they are legitimate requirements and don't violate other work rules or standards, they will pave the way for getting better performance from the employees, provided that we communicate these standards to the employee before he or she is asked to perform the duties.

Toby Wellman works for Bill Morris, the manager of engineering, and is the supervising engineer over the structural considerations. This entails taking remodeling or expansion plans from the design section and verifying that they are structurally sound. Once the plans are approved, the structure section "bird-dogs" the projects through to completion, keeping up with progress, making sure the proper materials are used, and seeing that building proceeds according to the design. The projects are assigned to one of several engineers or associate engineers who work for Toby. Typically, they work on three or four projects at a time. Depending on their complexity and their scheduled completion times, the projects are assigned either to experienced graduate engineers or to the less-qualified associate engineers who came up through the ranks of productions and were brought into engineering because of their experience more than their technical expertise. Right now Toby is having trouble with Jack Newhouse, an associate engineer.

Newhouse is a long-service employee who came into engineering from the building group, where he was an "expert" in cement and also in wall stress. He got to be good by watching and asking questions and he showed the ability to make decisions on his own. Lately his outlook toward his assignments has not appeared very good. Twice in one of his recent projects he has allowed work to be done contrary to design specifications, leading to delays in construction while the changes were ironed out. In addition to that, Jack spent considerable time arguing with the design engineers—and his boss Toby—over the plans. He contends that the way he approved the work to be done was just as good, or better, than the orginal design. While there is some validity to this, nothing but chaos would result if the structural engineering people were allowed to make such changes. A recent conversation between Toby and Jack went like this.

Toby: I understand that your way of doing this will work, Jack, but that's not the issue . . .

Jack: (Breaking in): No, that's *exactly* the issue! I've been through enough of these kinds of projects to know what will and won't work. The hotshot engineer who designed this has only his degree to point at—not experience.

Toby: That's still not the issue! What was designed was what was approved, what the materials were bought for, and what the crew was brought in to build; so that's the way we are going to build it . . .

Jack: (Again breaking in): Aw, come on! You mean we don't have any flexibility to change *anything at all*?

Toby: Jack, we've been through the procedures before. We can *recommend* the changes, but it has to go through me, then over to Al Bartow in design, and on to the originating engineer. Al gives the final okay on any changes.

Jack: Why can't I go directly to the design engineer on the job?

Toby: Well, technically you could, but I prefer knowing what you are doing; so I want you to come through me.

Jack: What about Alice Garth? She talks directly to her counterparts. Why does she have special privileges?

Toby: Uh, I don't think of it as special privileges. In the past she always has been right with everything she does, so I told her to go ahead and talk to the engineers in the other section, unless she needed help from me.

Toby has a number of problems with Jack Newhouse, and we'll need to deal with all of them. First, let's talk some more about standards. As it turns out, Toby has more than one set of standards; he has one set for Jack and another set for Alice Garth. Here we have both of the things we've been talking about. There are basic job standards which Jack knows, but the supervisor also has some personal standards for each of these two engineering people. There is no doubt that Jack knows the basic job standards; he has been informed of them on more than one occasion. In the second place, there seem to be some good reasons for having two sets of standards, but until now they *have not* been communicated very well.

Ideally, we will end up with standards that are oriented to the job, not to other employees. We should always be measuring the employees against the expected job performance. If we find ourselves comparing employees, our standards can soon get too high or too low. If we have all good performers, employees excelling normal expectations, we will conclude that a marginal or even satisfactory employee is well below standard because he or she is not doing as well as most of the high achievers. If we have set a reasonable set of standards for the job, it's easier to get a clear picture of the worth of the person, regardless of how well or poorly employees have done or are now doing the job.

Now we see that perhaps Toby is somewhat guilty of violating this rule of thumb regarding job standards. He has set up standards of performance based on what he would like everybody to do, though he doesn't expect, *or require,* that all employees meet this standard. He would like all employees to be good enough at their jobs that they could go directly to the engineers in the other section without coming through him. He probably sees Alice as the "good" employee and Jack as the "bad" one. But even Toby admits that technically Alice was not following the organization's procedures, but he justified it anyway on the fact that she was so good all the time. Note that there's nothing wrong in coming up with a new standard if we have capable employees, but we certainly

Removing Obstacles to Good Performance

To remove obstacles to good performing, technical managers should:

3. Orient standards to the *job,* not to other employees

can't judge Jack's performance on the basis of Alice's. Whether or not Jack is meeting standards in other ways does not make him a poor performer because he has to come to Toby for approval of changes. It would be interesting to ask Toby if Alice ever fails to meet the standards. He would probably say, "Oh, no! Not Alice! She's the one I depend on always to meet the requirements of the job." We can't quarrel with Toby about her performance, but we shouldn't make Jack bad when he is, in fact, meeting standards in this case. The rule is simple: when we hire an employee for a job (or move one to a job), we should be able to say, "A satisfactorily performing employee will be doing this and this and this. . . ." Then when others exceed that, they are just better than the standard; but they are not making someone else, who is actually meeting the standards, a below-standard performer.

As is always the case, standards must be communicated ahead of the performance time, but the employees also need to be trained if they're expected to perform adequately. This will definitely improve the possibilities of better performance. It's never fair to ask employees to perform tasks for which they're going to be evaluated without first seeing that they know how to perform that task. For example, if we're going to expect the employees to make formal presentations, or conduct meetings on some aspect of their jobs, they deserve the opportunity to learn how to make presentations or conduct meetings. If we don't do that, we certainly shouldn't hold poor performance against them!

Removing Obstacles to Good Performance

To remove obstacles to good performing, technical managers should:

4. Communicate standards ahead of performance time
5. Train employees to standard, as needed
6. Give employees feedback on their performance—while they are performing

A final aspect of paving the way for better performance is making sure that the employees have access to proper, reliable, and usable feedback on the way they are performing with respect to the standards we have communicated to them. *Simply put, they need to know how well they're doing.* There's never a reason to wait until formal appraisal time to do our evaluation of a person's performance, and there should certainly be no surprises at formal appraisal time. This is important from a motivation standpoint—if the employee is doing well—because he or she gets some very much-needed positive reinforcement. More than that, though, most employees want to do a good job; and if they aren't, they like to know it so they can improve. They also like to know that they're doing well, and if we tell them, they're more likely to continue to perform at the same level.

It's not a matter of constantly telling them how well or poorly they are doing; we don't look over their shoulders every moment of the day, saying, "That's good, that's bad, that's right, that's wrong." As we've seen with most technical and professional people, the less we look over their shoulders, the better they're likely to perform. We do, however, need to give them enough information and feedback on their performance that they'll know the direction they need to take—continue for good performance or alter course for poor performance. Ideally, this can be done at the completion of a project or of a phase of a long activity. It is best done in a short time without overkill; and while it needs to be formal enough to eliminate any doubt that we're giving valuable feedback, it isn't as formal as an appraisal interview. In this situation there is no advance work by the employee coming into the meeting on self-evaluation. Rather it's a matter of taking a few minutes to let the employee know how we feel about the performance to this point. There's nothing wrong—in fact, it might be advisable—in asking the employees how they feel about their work as of this moment. Since it's informal enough that there are no records kept of the feelings of either, there can be some disagreement, without it becoming an issue. The main thing is for the employee to know how we feel and to have a chance to contribute some to the informal appraisal.

INTERVIEWING THE POOR PERFORMER

As we've already discussed, there are many reasons why the employees need to know when they're not performing up to the standard we've set for them. The most obvious reason, though, is to improve the performance. As simple as that sounds, supervisors often lose sight of that fact and get involved in other reasons, such as "getting even" with the perpetrator, venting our emotions and frustrations, punishing the unsatisfactory employees, setting an example before the other workers, letting the employee know that "you can't get away with that around here," and others. Surprisingly enough, there is some validity to each of these ideas if they are not carried to the extreme. We do want to set an example for the others, to show that there are expectations and that it is not acceptable to fall short of the expectations. We do want to "punish" poor performers, to some extent, if that's the only way to get them to believe that we are serious about meeting standards. Of course, we have to be careful about letting our emotions get out of hand, and any kind of discipline done to relieve ourselves of frustrations, or even done in an emotional state, will always end in less than satisfactory circumstances. Again, the most legitimate reason for dealing with the unsatisfactory performer is to get a change in behavior, a change for the better.

There are some steps we should take in any interview, including the interview we have with the employee who is not meeting standards. After making sure that we have our facts and documentation in good order, and after we've picked a time and place that is conducive to an uninterrupted interview, we'll want to start off the interview by putting the employee at ease as much and as quickly as possible. Whether we're talking about the weather, sports, or family, a few words of friendly, if not too relaxed conversation will start things off unemotionally and allow us to deal with the facts at hand. The second step is to establish the purpose of this particular interview. There is no reason to "beat about the bush" on the matter. "It seems that this is a good time to discuss the results of the work you did on the last lab experiment." If we can, we should avoid saying things like, "I think we ought to talk about your poor performance." We'll want that to be clear momentarily, but the idea of "I think" makes it a one-way meeting, with only our opinions counting. Leading into the idea of "your poor performance" immediately sets the stage for hostility. One problem that technical and professional supervisors have is dealing with their misconceived notion that all their people want is straight, hard, undoctored truth, without any tact or softening. As it turns out, most high-tech people are just that: *people.* And being people, they act and react just like people do. They get defensive when they are criticized; they object to being told they are wrong; they get emotional

Interviewing the Poor Performer

To interview the poor performer, technical managers should take the following steps:

1. Have the documentation in order
2. Pick a time and place conducive to an uninterrupted interview
3. Put the employee at ease
4. Establish the purpose of the interview

when they think they're going to be punished in some way. In other words, they are almost disgustingly normal in these kinds of ways. They may not always *use* tact in dealing with people, but they respond quite well to it when it is used on them.

The next step is to establish some ground rules for conducting the interview and for the follow-up after the interview. Establishing the procedures may be no more than explaining that we'd like to let the employee know how we feel about the performance and get his or her idea of how they feel. It may include a statement of what we're looking for, perhaps a way to see that this mistake doesn't occur again or how we can cut down on the amount of overtime needed for doing this particular operation. As far as the procedure for what is going to be done after the interview, we may be talking about taking a look at the next project halfway through to make certain that the improvements are being instituted, or looking at the performance a month from now to see if we're meeting the agreed-upon objectives more closely.

As for the actual interview, we need to remember that we're talking to someone who is sensitive, intelligent, and for the most part, anxious to perform well. It isn't to be seen or conducted as a combat situation. It is two adults sitting down in a boss-subordinate arrangement, with the sole purpose of making sure that a specific job gets done in the manner it's designed to be done. There's no reason to complicate it with emotions or accusations. We should avoid the use of accusative expressions, such as "Why did you do it this way?" Neither are we looking for blame or excuses. If there is a legitimate reason why a thing wasn't done properly, then by all means we need to know that. If there is something blocking the performance as we'd like to see it be done, we should be alert to that and get as much information as possible. Mostly, though, we're going to be in situations where an employee isn't doing what should and could be done. In this interview, it is up to us to correct this deficiency. Finally, wherever possible and especially early in the interview, we will want to use open-ended questions in order to encourage participation by the employee. At some point we'll want to be direct enough that there is no doubt that we're talking about a specific problem and that we have the documentation about that problem. There should be a clear statement of the expectations—repeated as much as possible by the employee so we will know that the message was received—so that he or she leaves the interview with a clear understanding of what was said and with a time set for review of the performance that is going to be corrected.

The follow-up is as important as the interview itself. It is the time when the employee has a chance to remove the "demerits" of doing it incorrectly the first time. It allows the slate to be wiped clean enough to keep the problem from going further into the records or personnel files. It also serves as the time in which we can let the employee know *that we know* the job is being done correctly. It's essential feedback, both for assurance and positive reinforcement, and as a further training opportunity. At this time we can work on any fine points of the job that might need improvement with training. Of course, this is also the time when we may need to take some other action

Interviewing the Poor Performer

To interview the poor performer, technical managers should take the following steps:

5. Establish ground rules and procedures for conducting the interview and the follow-up
6. Allow the employee to remove "demerits" in the follow-up

because the employee has not improved or changed the behavior we are dissatisfied with. Although this isn't the goal of the followup, it is one of the advantages of having this scheduled follow-up. At least we will know and be able to deal with the problem quickly. Since we set the date and gave the employee time to change the behavior, there will be no reason to believe that we're simply "hounding" the employee when we do have the scheduled meeting or review.

TAKING DISCIPLINARY ACTION

As we've seen already, it's not very pleasant to get involved in dealing with the unsatisfactory employee. The very idea of discipline is repugnant to both supervisors and subordinates. Yet in the daily performing of the supervisory job, we must take action which is, in fact, discipline. Here, again, we're talking about some supervisory skills. If these skills are learned and applied, the job will be much easier. We need to think of discipline as a management tool that regulates the job performance and hence the outcome of the job itself. We've seen that the main goal of discipline is to improve performance, not "nail" the employee. It is the part of management that we include in the "controlling" function. It's the same thing as having meters and gauges and bells and whistles in a control room of a large operation. When we get some kind of signal, it means that something isn't functioning as it was designed to and that corrective action is needed. By taking the action while the activity is ongoing, instead of stopping everything until the adjustment is made (or waiting until the end and junking the the product), we can still get satisfactory results. When we see that an employee is not performing correctly and take action quickly to correct that performance, we can still have a satisfactory end product, that is, an employee doing the job as it's intended to be done. So we see that discipline is sometimes essential to getting the job done.

If there is a key disciplinary activity, it has to be documentation. More than one supervisor has ended up silly and ridiculous with a statement like, "You've been late too many times and we're going to have to take action." When the employee, either facetiously or seriously, asks, "How many times is too many times—and how many times have I been late?" the supervisor who has set no standards and has no documentation in hand is left with no legitimate answer. We can avoid this by keeping accurate records with dates and times. Sooner or later we will need that information if we plan any action to correct the poor performer. It takes time, and sometimes is a lot of trouble; but in the end, we can't do the job without this information.

Lacking the necessary documentation is only one of the several pitfalls that often confront us when we attempt to take disciplinary action. Another is being frightened or wanting to avoid the embarrassment of an emotional scene. Usually, people who think like this either are expecting things to be much worse than they are in reality, or have done a poor job of supervising in the past and are rightfully expecting the results of such supervision. As long as supervisors act like mature people, the results should never get out of hand. The supervisor sets the stage; the subordinates most often follow that lead. Another pitfall is inconsistency in enforcing the rules. Just as we are in trouble if we don't have the proper documentation, we also will have a serious problem if we impose discipline on some people but not on others or if we impose different discipline for the same infraction or the same discipline for different degrees of infraction. Employees have a right to expect us to be consistent, and we have an obligation to give management above us a consistent operation in our area of influence. One reason we sometimes appear to be inconsistent is that we allow things to go too far and then overreact. We let employees continue to perform unsatisfactorily, and then, either because someone calls our hand on it or we get tired of it, we strike out at the first person who violates the rules or doesn't meet the standards. Discipline needs to be as close to the infraction as possible, but it should still be done with a level head and with reason and thought behind it. There are times, too, when we just plain play favorites. It is easy to get along with employees who have good attitudes—we either overlook the infractions or give lighter disciplinary actions—whereas it is also easy to watch more closely and deal swiftly and more harshly with employees who aren't so easy to get along with.

Often supervisors fail to take steps in discipling employees for fear that higher management will not support them in the action. In some cases, that's a legitimate point; but for the most part, there is generally a reason why management doesn't support these actions, if indeed they don't. The usual reason is that the supervisor has failed to properly document the actions that led to the discipline. It is also possible that what we plan in some way interferes with a more important part of the work agreement negotiations. Usually, these can be explained ahead of time, and most often there isn't a problem in the first place. We can and should have management support for the actions we want to take, provided that the action is in keeping with management policy and philosophy. If

Taking Disciplinary Action

When taking disciplinary action, technical managers should:

1. Use discipline as a management tool
2. Take corrective action quickly while the activity is going on
3. Use documentation skillfully

we do our part correctly, this support will come without much problem.

Perhaps the most certain way of getting support is to have the consistency we just talked about. If we have the reputation for always dealing fairly and accurately with nonperformance, both management and the subordinates will respect and support us in what we're doing. As we will continue to see, documentation will go a long way toward getting this reputation across. When we go to higher management with proper documentation of our story, we have a good chance of getting whatever support we need. However, if we go ill-prepared, with less-than-tangible evidence, we're in trouble from the beginning. We have no right to ask management to support something on just our word that the employee did certain things when we have no evidence or corroboration. It's not a matter of trust: it's more a matter of asking management to set a precedent of supporting action for which there has been no reliable, documented evidence.

If we aren't careful, we will put management in a difficult role of having to support us when we may not really deserve it. We fail to keep them informed, ask them to support us without documentation, and expect them to take our side in disputes or negotiations without having given them very good tools to argue with; we put them on the spot by saying that we will lose our respect if they don't stand behind us, even though we've been consistently inconsistent! We also tend to look at the decisions they make in terms of how they affect us, in our span of control, rather than looking at what we and they do in light of what it will mean in *their* sphere of influence or of how it will perhaps influence the entire organization. A little empathy on our part will go a long way toward building more understanding of their considerations.

KEEPING MANAGEMENT INFORMED

Part of the whole support effort we are asking for is our keeping management informed as to what is going on in our department or group. While we are likely to do this in things like production, safety, or even turnover or waste, we are less likely to do it with things like poor performers and individual disciplinary action. It isn't out job to pass every event up the line, nor is it higher management's job to try to know everything that is going on, but there is a middle ground of information sharing that will help all who are concerned. For example, if we have an employee who was highly recruited because of seeming to have great potential but who just isn't measuring up to the standards we have a right to expect, we need to share that information with higher management—because of the interest that was shown in this person from the beginning. This will avoid any surprises if serious discipline is required. It will also gain us some support if we feel that the employee either needs more time to develop or is in the wrong slot as far as job assignment is concerned.

When we're dealing with professional and technical people in areas where there is less tangible evidence of satisfactory work, management can assist us greatly in setting standards and finding ways of measuring these standards. Because there is sometimes a lack of tangible performance, such as

Keeping Management Informed

To keep management informed, technical managers should:

1. Avoid giving management too many details
2. Inform to prevent surprises
3. Let management help in setting standards for less tangible work areas
4. Use management's help on raises, promotions, and discharges
5. Stick by their decisions but learn from them

designing software or coming up with innovative ideas, the middle management people may have to make some decisions about what is or isn't satisfactory. They can best do this when we supply them with as much tangible evidence as possible which they can use to go to the more subjective areas. This is true, of course, not only when we're talking about possible discipline, but also in other areas, such as promotions, bonuses, and general performance appraisals. As we've seen over and over, somebody somewhere can make a decision as to what it is worth to keep a person and when it is no longer worth it for the person to continue performing as he or she is.

LIVING WITH OUR DECISIONS

After we've made the decisions to discipline employees, using whatever standards and whatever measuring we want to use, we are obligated to stick by our decisions as much as we can. This doesn't mean that we stand behind an obviously incorrect decision: but in the long run, we're better off not turning back after we've decided to take a certain action. By all means we should try to learn from the decision we've made by watching the consequences carefully. Part of getting the reputation for consistency is sticking with the decisions we've made unless there is a legitimate appeal which shows where we have erred.

Sometimes it's not so much a matter of not sticking by the decision as it is grieving over it, wondering if it was the right thing to do, regretting it, wondering if we should change it, and generally being miserable as the activity works its way out to completion. As we've seen, learning from the decisions is important, but dwelling on it beyond reason is a grave mistake. When we have done the best we know and have made the decision to take the action, it becomes like any other decision we make; we live with it the best we can! There is a way of approaching it that will help. We should remember that there is no way we can ever say if we had done something in another way, we would have gotten a specific result instead. It just doesn't work that way. Having taken one fork of the decision, there is no power in us or anyone else that can tell us what would have happened if we'd taken the other fork. We can all speculate, but that's all it is. Knowing this, we are better off leaving it alone than wishing we had taken a different route.

CONCLUSION

Since discipline is a proven tool of managing the job and managing people, the successful supervisor must on occasion resort to it. There are some skills involved, and they can be learned. There are some specific steps we can take that will make discipline easier for us. Those who use discipline find that it is most often so effective that its use quickly reduces the need for it. People realize that we are serious about getting the job done and getting it done according to the expectations of the organization. Seeing us use discipline when there are those who fail to meet the expectations will cause our employees to respect us, and they will try more diligently to meet the standards themselves. This, of course, assumes that we are doing a good job of practicing the disciplinary skills.

Removing Obstacles to Good Performance

To remove obstacles to good performance, technical managers should:

1. Set good job standards, approved by the organization
2. Identify acceptable, personal standards of the supervisor
3. Orient standards to the *job,* not to other employees
4. Communicate standards ahead of performance time
5. Train employees to standard, as needed
6. Give employees feedback on their performance—while they are performing

Interviewing the Poor Performer

To interview the poor performer, technical managers should take the following steps:

1. Have the documentation in order
2. Pick a time and place conducive to an uninterrupted interview
3. Put the employee at ease
4. Establish the purpose of the interview
5. Establish ground rules and procedures for conducting the interview and the follow-up
6. Allow the employee to remove "demerits" in the follow-up

Taking Disciplinary Action

When taking disciplinary action, technical managers should:

1. Use discipline as a management tool
2. Take corrective action quickly while the activity is going on
3. Use documentation skillfully

Keeping Management Informed

To keep management informed, technical managers should:

1. Avoid giving management too many details
2. Inform to prevent surprises
3. Let management help in setting standards for less tangible work areas
4. Use management's help on raises, promotions, and discharges
5. Stick by their decisions but learn from them

chapter eleven

How Should I Develop Information for Technical Updates?

INTRODUCTION

Perhaps we should delete the word "technical" in the chapter title. Neither managers nor employees seem to like surprises—technical or otherwise. Of course there are times (like the shift in priorities we discussed) when a situation catches Matt himself by surprise. And he doesn't like being caught off guard, either. So he makes a special effort to get and give relevant information to key people continuously. Who are the key people? What is the relevant information?

Matt's supervisor is one of the key people, of course. But in different situations the informed support of other people can be critical. In a given situation, four people are likely to be especially important:

The Official Decision Maker. This person is usually easy enough to spot. Through channels, this person should hear whatever official policy prescribes and sometimes—but not always—more.

The Opinion Leader. This person may be more difficult to identify. This is the person whose opinion the official decision maker is likely to accept. Sometimes an official decision maker may actually adopt the decision of a trusted secretary, a regular drinking buddy, a golfing partner, or a protegé. And since "opinion leader" is an unofficial role, information with this person is best exchanged informally—at the water fountain, on a coffee break, on the golf course. When the opinion leader is inaccessible informally, his information needs can be included in the official channel that goes to the decision maker.

The Gatekeeper. The gatekeeper controls the flow of information between the originator and the decision maker. In a conflict between Matt's department and Jim Swales (vice president for operations), for example, Matt's supervisor could control Matt's access to Swales—the frequency and the quality.

The Consumer. The consumer is the person or the organization who will use the goods or services decisions are being made about. It's often critical to involve the consumer in setting parameters and laying out specifications *up front.* Early consumer involvement can help minimize the risks of becoming trapped in a deadlock as Janice and Matt seemed to be with Swales.

One large consumer products company budgeted $250,000 for a new computer-based personnel information system. The project was expected to take nine months. But $2.5 million and two years later the project was abandoned: $3.6 million more was needed to complete it. What happened? The consumer (the director of human resources) de-

Developing Information for Technical Updates

To effectively develop information for technical updates, technical managers should:

1. Know where to find the key people for a given project
2. Sift through data for information
3. Spell out who relates to whom and how

cided that his staff's involvement was a waste of time, so he pulled them off the project. The information systems manager tried to push the project through to completion anyway. With no guidance—but lots of pressure—from the human resources staff, he redesigned and redesigned the project in an effort to "cover" every possibility. Inevitably, the project collapsed of its own weight (McFarlan, 1981, pp. 142, 148).

KNOW WHERE TO FIND THE KEY PEOPLE FOR A GIVEN PROJECT

Whenever there is only loose agreement on the outcomes for an activity or whenever those outcomes seem poorly defined, Matt is especially careful to keep in touch with the people outside his own staff—his supervisor, of course, but also the chain of command above his supervisor. And loosely agreed on outcomes require continuous, concrete dialogue with the client inside or outside the organization (as Matt found in his relationship with Jim Swales).

On the other hand, when his people have a higher level of experience with the technology of a project, Matt gives extra attention to the key people on his own staff. Oddly enough, the least challenging projects have been the ones endangered most by infighting in his own group. Matt sometimes steps in to perform the "gatekeeper" function himself. But his example of gatekeeping is often picked up by some member of the team who becomes a kind of "third-party negotiator" for opposing factions. Otherwise, when interpersonal conflicts keep a team stirred up, it's easy for someone with critical information to withdraw mentally and leave important facts unsaid.

SIFT THROUGH DATA FOR INFORMATION

The volume of data in even a short project can be overwhelming. In fact, it can numb people in the management chain to the point that they simply no longer hear it or see it. So it's critical that a technical manager sift through the reams of data for worthwhile information to pass up the chain of command. What's the difference between information and data? By definition information *informs* someone; data may or may not. To sift data for information, Matt asks himself three questions:

1. What do I expect the receiver to do, think, or feel differently as a result of having this information?
2. What *must* that person know in order to do, think, or feel what I expect?
3. What would help that person better understand or better accept the information I'm passing on?

If data helps answer one of these questions, Matt's information would be incomplete without it. If data doesn't answer one of these questions, it will only "clutter" Matt's reporting and detract from the relevant information. When circumstances change, today's data may become tomorrow's information. So Matt throws no data away: he stores it where it can be easily retrieved—by him or by a subordinate.

SPELL OUT RELATIONSHIPS AND GIVE NEEDED INFORMATION TO EACH KEY PERSON

Because line authority becomes blurred when technical experts are involved, one of the most confusing questions in a technical project is:

Who relates to whom and how?

This question is so important and the answer is often so confusing that many technical managers use a *linear responsibility chart* to make the answer clear. (For a detailed explanation of the procedure, you may want to consult the excellent article by Donald W. Barnes in the July 1972 issue of *Industrial Engineering*: Linear responsibility charting, July 1972, pp. 17–19.)

The *development* of a linear responsibility chart often does more to clarify tasks and relationships than does the final chart itself. The development requires team leaders and team members to identify the roles of key people in each function of a project:

Who authorizes a task?
Who coordinates with other parts of organization?
Who supervises the task?

______________ Project

Linear Responsibility Chart

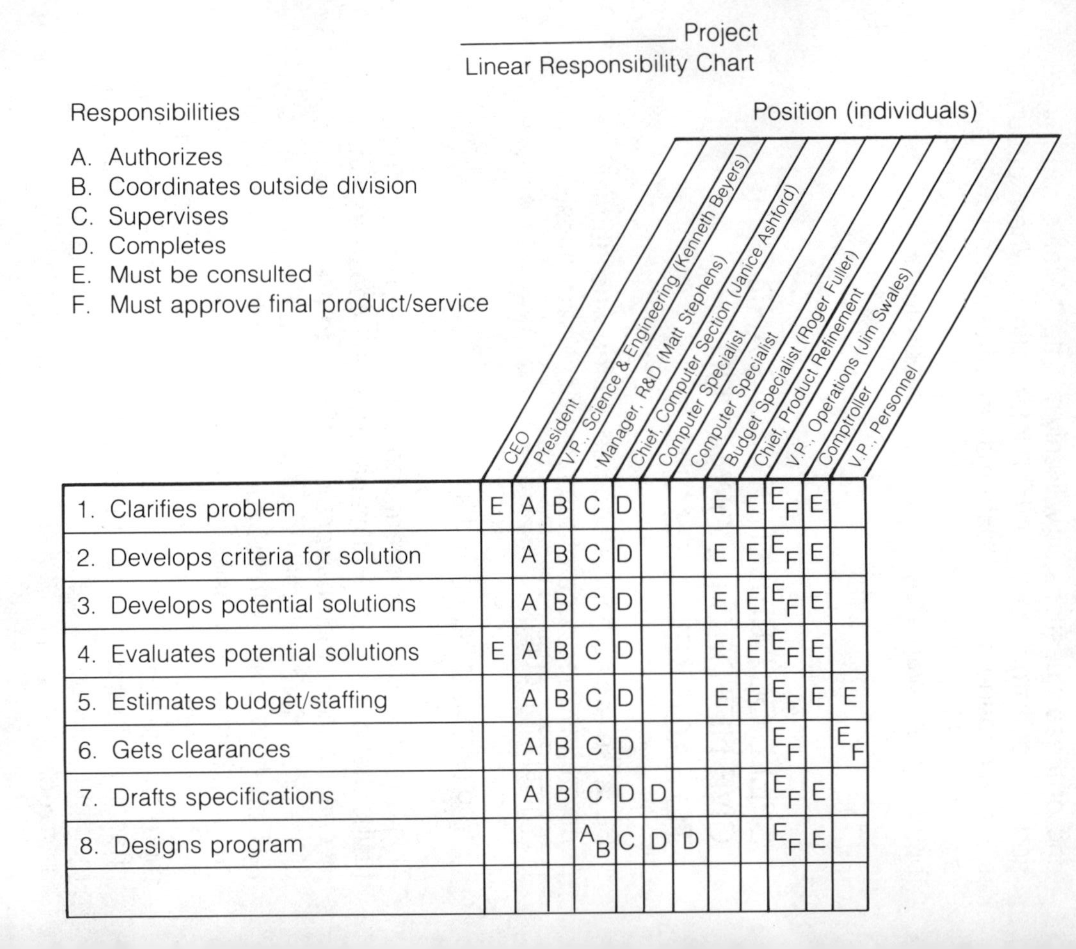

Responsibilities

A. Authorizes
B. Coordinates outside division
C. Supervises
D. Completes
E. Must be consulted
F. Must approve final product/service

Position (individuals)

	CEO	President	V.P., Science & Engineering (Kenneth Beyers)	Manager, R&D (Matt Stephens)	Chief, Computer Section (Janice Ashford)	Computer Specialist	Computer Specialist	Budget Specialist (Roger Fuller)	Chief, Product Refinement	V.P., Operations (Jim Swales)	Comptroller	V.P., Personnel
1. Clarifies problem	E	A	B	C	D			E	E	E_F	E	
2. Develops criteria for solution		A	B	C	D			E	E	E_F	E	
3. Develops potential solutions		A	B	C	D			E	E	E_F	E	
4. Evaluates potential solutions	E	A	B	C	D			E	E	E_F	E	
5. Estimates budget/staffing		A	B	C	D			E	E	E_F	E	E
6. Gets clearances		A	B	C	D					E_F		E_F
7. Drafts specifications		A	B	C	D	D				E_F	E	
8. Designs program				A_B	C	D	D			E_F	E	

Who actually completes the task?

Who must be consulted (technical or administrative specialists)?

Who must approve the final product/service?

A good task analysis or operations manual may be the original source of steps in a given project. But before it is finished a useful chart spells out *what actually happens*—not always the same as what's written in a manual. The chart on the preceding page will serve as an example.

Matt's dilemma with Jim Swales (remember Chapter 4) illustrates the value of developing a linear responsibility chart: many of the problems could have been prevented if Matt had insisted on input from and approval by Swales during the early phases of the project.

CONCLUSION

It's important to keep key people informed. But they're likely to be overloaded with data already. And even without overload, a message can be clouded or distorted by unclear relationships between team members.

Developing Information for Technical Updates

To effectively develop information for technical updates, technical managers should:

1. Know where to find the key people for a given project
2. Sift through data for information
3. Spell out who relates to whom and how

chapter twelve

How Should I Deliver Technical Presentations?

INTRODUCTION

Al Burton, the supervisor of the design section has to make a presentation as a result of a new design that he and his group have come up with through some of their studies. The audience is a group of local university technical students who are all members of a chapter of the local design engineers. Al is concerned because he's not a speechmaker and is talking to Denise, who has had some speaking experience.

Al: This is a new experience for me, and frankly I'm scared.

Denise: Well, I can understand your stage fright. I remember the first time I made a presentation before a large audience.

Al: I'm not so sure that it's stage fright when I say I'm scared; I guess more than anything else I'm afraid I'm going to be received like some of the other speakers I've heard at these chapter meetings.

Denise: What do you mean?

Al: Well, I never thought of it from the speaker's side, but sitting in the audience I find that some of these things are extremely dull if you're not actually working on the project or involved in it in some way.

Denise: So you're frightened that you won't come across very well.

Al: Yes, I am. I've worked a lot on the material, so I'm certainly not concerned about knowledge of the subject.

Denise: Well, at least you do know your subject, and that ought to be a lot of help and encouragement.

Al: Well, it doesn't really help very much as far as the concern I have about being a bad speaker. I've tried it a few times here in the company; and frankly, I haven't been very successful.

Denise: How do you know you've been bad?

Al: Well, it seems to me that people just look and act bored; some of them seem to go into a daze when I start to speak. As I compare myself to other people, I think I know who's good and who's bad.

Denise: Well, I think we all have that kind of a feeling when we first get started, especially those in the technical areas.

Al: I know you've had some training in this area. Can you help me some?

Denise: I can give you some pointers. You can learn to speak, and there are some good courses available to help you.

Al: It's too late for that because my presentation is a week from Monday.

Denise: Let me start off by giving you something to think about. There are three things that you have to work out, and I would think that you've already done at least part of it. The first is to know your topic. Second, you must know your audience. Third, you have to know yourself. Therein lies the success or failure of most presentations.

Al has a familiar problem. Technical people usually aren't prepared to make presentations, and many of them aren't very good at it. Al does have the advantage of knowing his subject, but that's nearly always true of technical people. In fact, they spend most of their time on the technical material rather than on the presentation itself. It's good that Al is, at this point, beginning to decide that it's not just the knowledge of the subject that's going to get him through. There are some speaking habits that he will have to develop, and he will have to worry about his audience.

KNOW THE TOPIC

Denise gave him some good advice. She suggested that he first *know the topic.* Let's look at some implications of knowing the topic. First, obviously, it means that we should be an expert in the field we have chosen to talk about and should be prepared to answer at least a certain number of questions from the audience. We must know the topic well enough to outline it and should organize the material with an outline of some kind, going back to review the outline and to reoutline and reorganize it. After doing this a couple of times, it wouldn't hurt to put it aside for a day and then get it out and look at it, asking the question, "If I were doing this for the very

Preparing for a Technical Presentation

To prepare for a technical presentation, technical managers should:

1. Know the topic

first time, is this the way I would organize it?" Sooner or later we have to decide that this is the best organization we can get and start putting the meat on the outline.

After we get an outline we feel we can live with, we need to ask ourselves what kinds of questions the audience is likely to ask and what kinds of questions we would like them to ask, and if we have the information or backup data to answer those questions. We can pretty well get an idea of the kinds of questions they'll ask based on the kind of presentation we make. If we emphasize or raise doubts about certain things or make some points more interesting than others, there's a good chance that our questions will come from those areas. Perhaps the best thing we can know about the subject is what we

Know Your Topic

Knowing your topic means to:

1. Know the subject well enough to outline it
2. Consider questions the audience might ask and be prepared with information
3. Decide on certain areas of the topic on which you just don't have expertise
4. Determine what these people need to take away with them

don't know about it. We have to know what we know, organize what we know, and decide on certain areas of the subject that we just don't have expertise in. If a question does come up in these areas, we can very quickly say: I'm sorry, but that's not my field," or "I'm sorry, you'll have to ask someone else," or "I really don't feel confident to give a good answer on that."

The next step is to ask ourselves: What is our purpose? What do we really want these people to take away with them after this meeting is over? What we're really saying is that we know that they're not going to remember everything we say, but they might remember one or two or three key points. In the beginning, we need to ask ourselves which of these points we want them to remember. These are the ones we should emphasize, have examples for, use visuals with, and make sure that they can handle to some degree after our presentation.

KNOW THE AUDIENCE

This brings us to the second thing that Denise suggested, which was to *know the audience.* If possible, there are some things that we have to find out about the people we're speaking to, even while we're developing the material and organizing our outline. We need to ask such simple questions as, "Why are they there?" "What can I do to capture their attention?" "What can I promise them in the presentation that will interest them?" and "What is their listening and information tolerance?" First, when we ask, "Why are they there?," we need to know if they are there of their own accord, if they are there to meet some requirement, or if they're there because somebody sent them. Each one of these things will make a difference in how we make our presentation. If they're there because they are excited, are interested in the subject, or want to learn about that subject because they need the information, obviously, they are going to listen a lot more closely, and we'll have to do a little bit less in selling them on the importance of the subject. On the other hand, if they are there because somebody sent them or required them to be there, we'll have to do a little better selling job and not go as deeply into the subject as we would otherwise.

Regardless of how they got there, we need to think of some things that they're interested in so that we can capture their attention early in the presentation. We can tell a story of some kind that relates to the subject; we can relate an interesting event that's happened to us which points out the importance of this material; we can show how our own void as far as this information is concerned might have caused us a problem in some way. Part of the selling is to make a promise. This is really the same thing that we meant earlier when we asked, "What do I want them to take away from the presentation?" What we really say to them is: "When you leave this presentation, here are some questions that you'll be able to answer, or here are some things that you'll know, or here are some relationships that you can explain." Finally, when we ask the question about their listening and information tolerance, we have to know if they are going to come to us after sitting all day long listening to somebody else, or if they've come in from work into a warm room, or if they are used to this kind of presentation and are able to sit for some period of time concentrating on what's being said. We need to know something about their educational or informational level—just how deep they can go, how much tolerance they have for thinking about things, and how well they can put things together and process information. If they're not used to doing these things, their reception of our presentation is going to suffer, but if we know these things about them, we can do a better job of organizing the material and preparing the presentation so that they'll get the most good from it.

KNOW YOURSELF

The third thing that Denise suggested to Al was that he should *know himself.* This is an important aspect, particularly to Al, because most of his experience, training, and background are in technical material rather than in thinking about more abstract things, such as his appearance and how he will be perceived by the audience. This ought to become a confidence-building experience before the presentation starts. Al needs to convince himself that he really knows the subject, but at the same time he ought to recognize that there are some things that he can't answer. He ought to be able to say things like, "I'm sorry but that's not my field of expertise," or "That's an interesting question, and I'm going to do some more research on it, I'm glad you asked." He should know the topic well enough to be able to answer questions, but he also needs to know himself well enough to know how best to answer the questions. He needs to practice, perhaps even with role-playing kinds of questions that could be asked. These could be recorded and played on a tape while the speaker stands in front of the mirror and answers the questions. This is all part of the preparation.

The three basic rules for any speaker are simple enough. They are prepare, prepare, and prepare. The mirror is as good a place as any to prepare for the actual presentation. If

Preparing for a Technical Presentation

To prepare for a technical presentation, technical managers should:

2. Know the audience

3. Know themselves

we are going to be using notes, we can still stand in front of the mirror, because if we're familiar with the notes, we won't have to spend all of the time looking down. As we stand in front of the mirror, we can notice various objects in the room behind us; and this is the same thing as looking at the audience. It is a good idea to get a watch into the picture, too, so that we can know how long the presentation is going to be. Once we have prepared ourselves and are pretty sure that we know the subject, the audience, and ourselves, we should have confidence enough to make the presentation.

MAKING AN EFFECTIVE PRESENTATION

Now, let's notice some things that should happen during that presentation that will make it effective. First, when we go to the speaker's stand, or climb the steps to the stage, or just stand up in the seat where we are, we have to look confident. If we prepared ourselves well enough and built our confidence well enough, we can carry this off. Remember that this is going to be our first impression on the group and we should make it a positive one. We should take firm steps, stand straight, and act confident while we put our notes down or pull them out of our briefcase or sort the cards that are before us. While we're doing this, we should look at the group with all the air of confidence that we can show. If we sort of straggle to the speaker stand, look down at our notes, fumble around and take things out of our pockets, shuffle through the notes a little bit, and fail to look at the audience, we're going to give a pretty poor appearance and they will not think of us as being very confident.

The next thing we want to do is to *stay* confident. We not only look confident when we get up and act confident when we start, but we also need to have notes to ourselves along the way that say, "Stay confident!" One of the ways to show our confidence is to spend a lot of time looking at the audience. We look people in the eye, we look around to different groups, and we make our points looking straight at somebody. The other half of this is that we can also lose confidence this way by looking at someone who doesn't look interested. We may begun to wonder if she represents the whole audience or if she's getting bored. The key here is not to spend much time looking at those kinds of people but rather to move quickly to somebody else. If we can find three or four friendly faces in the audience, we need to concentrate on them. If the rest of the audience can see our eyes moving from one side of the room to the other, from the front to the back, the fact that we don't look them directly in the eye doesn't mean that we aren't confident or that they're not a part of the audience. The worst thing that we can do is to start to lose confidence by looking at somebody who looks discouraged or disinterested. We get panicky and start depending more and more on our notes, and our presentation becomes more boring. Then we look up, we see more people who are bored, and before it's over, this downward spiral will take us to some black hole of oblivion.

The next thing we have to consider during the presentation is our body language. This simply refers to how we stand and to the motions we have with our hands and our heads. If we're going to write on the easel, for example, we ought to make positive steps toward it. We ought to write with firmness and speed, and we ought to put the chalk or the pen down and move back to the speaker stand. We should avoid looking disinterested in our own motions; we want to be sort of "bigger than life" in our presentation.

Remember that our audience expects us to deal with technical things, and to have facts and figures; it does not expect us to be a golden-tongued orator. We shouldn't get the idea that we have to be dramatic in a technical presentation. When we talk about using body language, we are simply saying that if a point needs to be made, it's a good idea to emphasize that point not only with the words and the voice we use, but also by holding up one finger, counting on our hands, or somehow indicating that this is a point, and then here's another point and then here's another point.

We mentioned it once, but let's point out again that our words and our voices are somewhat like writing; we can use our tone to punctuate a sentence and a flow of words as a means of letting the group know that this is time to stop and think or this is an important issue. We can punctuate with the voice, by raising it and then stopping at the end of the sentence. We can put a dash or a comma in the voice with a delay or a pause. Sometimes we can be as effective by being quiet as we can by being loud. If we are speaking in a relatively soft tone and we suddenly pause, slow down, or lower the voice, the emphasis can be rather dramatic. Of course, these are the kinds of things we need to practice before we get up to speak.

We've already indicated that we ought to start with an air of confidence. One of the things that will help us do this is a good solid opening. As we begin, let the audience know that they're going to leave this presentation with some information; make the promises and then go right into doing what we've promised. The key is to say what we want to get said, and most audiences would rather we'd do that than regale them with stories and jokes. One of the reasons we have to use funny stories and jokes is that we haven't been able to make our material interesting enough. If this is the case, perhaps we need to spend time working on our presentation instead of looking for funny stories.

When we have had a good solid opening, presented the material in a logical way, and have made the points clear, we need a good, solid close. If we feel that a summary is important, we can do one; but this should not be a repeat of the speech. It is simply a way to close the presentation. It may be no more than saying, "So, basically, we have these three things" or "We have made these five points, which bring us to this conclusion." The conclusion ought to be one solid sentence, after which we sit down. As to what will be remembered, the ending is perhaps more important than either the beginning or the middle. If we do a good job of summarizing, make our point quickly, and sit down, the audience is going to be impressed enough to think that we really knew what we were doing and that we also knew when we were through doing it.

If there is to be a questioned-and-answer period after the presentation, it is still a good idea to sit down when the speech is over so that the audience will know that this is the end of what we had prepared to say. Even if we offer the audience a chance to ask questions, we might do this by addressing the chairperson ahead of time to let that be known and then sit down after thanking the audience and turning it back over to the chairperson. The chairperson can then offer the opportunity for people to ask questions. One reason for doing this is that the chairperson knows what the time schedule is and will be able to determine if there is time enough for questions. It is important to say what we have to say and to sit

Suggestions for an Effective Presentation

During the presentation, you should:

1. Look and act confident
2. Use good body language
3. Deliver a solid opening and closing

down when we are through. That distinguishes that part of the presentation from the off-the-cuff question time. When the questions come, the most important thing for us to remember is to deal directly with that question. It's a good idea to repeat the question. This will give us time to think about it and will also help assure us that we're talking about the right material. We might say something like, "As I understand it, you're asking so and so." This gives us the time to process the information, so that we can answer it in as few sentences as possible. If we have not completely covered the answer, the person will still have a chance to ask an additional question. We're a lot better off giving less rather than too much information. We can always fill in when there's a shortage, but there's no way we can take away from too much talking. The more time we spend before we answer the question, the less time it will take us to answer it. Remember what we said earlier: if we don't know the answer, we should not try to give one. It's a lot better to admit that we don't know than to try to answer the question and let the audience find out from all the things we say which don't apply that we don't know the answer.

Since we're talking about technical presentations, let's make some observations about the nature of this speech or talk. First, it will be filled with facts and figures, maybe charts and graphs. Just because our audience may be used to technical presentations, even lectures and long speeches without any visuals, doesn't mean that our presentation can't be improved with the use of some good visual aids. If we're going to talk about percentages, it's a good idea to have a bar graph or pie chart to illustrate this. We can use an overhead projector, or a slide, or maybe even draw an illustration on the board or on a paper easel. We shouldn't get the idea that because the audience is technical we are spoon-feeding them or somehow sugarcoating the material when we make it colorful by using good illustrations and assisting their learning and retention with an appeal to senses other than just their hearing. If the audience happens not to be technical, we have yet another problem. We have to make sure that what we say is understood by a nontechnical audience. This means that we will have to do away with the gobbledygook or jargon of the trade and use only ordinary words that the regular population can understand. Remember, we want them to hear and understand us, so we shouldn't ask them to work hard at figuring out the definitions of the words we're using. If there is a simpler way of presenting the material, explaining a subject or naming something, we should always go with the simpler term.

CONCLUSION

What have we said? We have said that making a technical presentation means that we need to know the subject, know the audience, and know ourselves. No matter how much we know the subject, our presentation will be better if we practice ahead of time. During the presentation we want to project an air of confidence which comes from having studied the audience, the material, and ourselves. We want to remember that we're making a technical presentation and that not everyone

Preparing for a Technical Presentation

To prepare for a technical presentation, technical managers should:

1. Know the topic
2. Know the audience
3. Know themselves

is as interested in that material as we are. When we have made the presentation and the curtain comes down on it, we would do well to go back and in our own mind look at what we did to see how we could improve. If it is taped so that we can listen to ourselves, that's a good way to see what we did. If we're honest enough to come home and take a look in that same mirror and to see where we can improve, this will ensure that we will do a better job next time, no matter how good we were this time.

Know Your Topic

Knowing your topic means to:

1. Know the subject well enough to outline it
2. Consider questions the audience might ask and be prepared with information
3. Decide on certain areas of the topic in which you just don't have expertise
4. Determine what these people need to take away with them

Suggestions for an Effective Presentation

During the presentation, you should:

1. Look and act confident
2. Use good body language
3. Deliver a solid opening and closing

chapter thirteen

How Should I Conduct Technical Meetings?

INTRODUCTION

Meetings have a bad name. Many people complain because they have to go to meetings, and many people dread even thinking about meetings; but any organization, especially a technical one, needs to have meetings. Perhaps their unpopularity has more to do with the way they are conducted than the fact that they exist. In this chapter we try to show that good technical meetings can be conducted efficiently and can have a high productivity. First, let's point out that any meeting should have a purpose. We can establish that there are a limited number of reasons or purposes why meetings are held (see box). We note these briefly now and go into more detail later.

Not only should a meeting have a purpose, but we should also have some goals when we conduct one. One of the primary reasons we conduct technical meetings is to make certain that everyone knows what the particular action is on a certain project or activity. Frequently, the meetings are held

Reasons for Holding a Meeting

Following are good reasons for conducting meetings:

1. To inform or report
2. To persuade or sell
3. To organize or reconstruct
4. To get information or ideas
5. To brainstorm or solve problems
6. To meet some requirements

so that certain actions can be assigned. Another goal we strive for in a meeting is to get commitment from people on a particular project. As we'll see later, that becomes very critical because it sets a pattern for how we're conducting the meeting. It is never *my* meeting, it is always *our* meeting. Finally, one of the goals we should have in a meeting is to get closure on a certain phase of the project so that we can move on toward the next phase of that activity.

In this chapter we talk about several things:

1. Preparing for the meeting
2. Conducting the meeting
3. Concluding the meeting
4. Following up on the meeting
5. Why meetings fail

SUCCESSFUL MEETINGS

Too often we go to a meeting and hear the chairperson saying things like, "What I want to see in this meeting is" or "I appreciate your coming to my meeting today, and I need some information from you." That kind of statement is really saying that the chairperson has a problem and the rest of us have been taken from our busy schedule to solve his or her problem. It is pretty sure that we rarely get very committed either to solving the problem or to enacting the solution when the chairperson doesn't make it "our" meeting as opposed to "my" meeting. As soon as possible, though, we need to establish the fact that this is a team effort with one person chosen to conduct the meeting but with the expectation that everybody will contribute to the meeting. Even in the introduction the statement should be made that, in essence, "We're all in this together." There may be even some reference to this in the announcement of the meeting that is sent out ahead of time.

Another thing that we can do ahead of time is assign different roles to the participants who attend the meeting. In the initial announcement, we can have a personal note to each participant, saying something like, "Sue, I'd like you to pay particular attention to the budget aspect of this project and be prepared to discuss that in the meeting" and "Charles, we are going to have some technical questions about the structure; and if you could bring some of the background information and be prepared to talk about it, it sure would be helpful." Even when the meeting starts, we can make additional assignments if that is at all possible. Most often we want to let the people know that we have made these assignments by saying in the introduction, "I have asked Sue to deal with some of the budget matters since that's her field, and Charles is going to talk to us about the structural design questions, if you have any." We can make additional assignments by calling on certain people to keep track of the time, serve as recorder, and do our summarizing for us. If no one chooses to play the devil's advocate, we may even assign that role during the meeting. We can say something like, "Bud, I know this has always been one of your pet peeves. How does what we're doing strike you?"

One of the most obvious things we should do but perhaps most often we fail to do is let the participants know that this meeting is also going to meet some of their needs. If we know that someone has a particularly good idea, we should make sure that this idea comes to the forefront. If we know that someone has some conflict in doing something the particular way we're going to do it, we need to make sure that person gets a chance to speak. When we sense that there is a degree of hostility between two or three of the members, we should take steps to correct this during the meeting if we can. As we'll see later, we can't always meet everyone's needs. There are some who have come with hidden agendas that may or may not get out in the open. We may not even know what they are; nevertheless, we need to let them know that this is their meeting as well as ours, and that they have as much right to participate and meet their own needs as we do.

Another successful philosophy is that as chairperson of a meeting we appreciate the help of those who participate and let them know that we do by keeping the meeting from going too long. It also helps to convince them that their help, as well as their time, is valuable, if we limit the extraneous activities, such as a long break, idle conversation, or a delay while we wait for those who are late.

Another basic philosophy for having successful meetings is that we never go into the meeting with all the answers figured out. Unless it is absolutely necessary, we need to be careful about "telling" them what's going to happen. It is bad to call a group of people together and tell them what's going to be after they thought they were going to contribute something. It's even worse to call them together, have them make their contribution, and *then* tell them the way it is going to be. It's all right for us to have some preconceived notions; everybody's going to come with some of those. It's all right for us to have some biases, because everyone will have some of those. But it's not all right for us to have a completely closed mind as far as what the end product is going to be like. The only time we would be in a position to tell them what's going to happen is when a positive decision has been made by someone with enough authority to do it, and we have been assigned the task of telling this committee or group of participants what has been decided. If a policy decision has already been made, we might do just as well to send out a memorandum or policy statement rather than calling people together to tell them.

Finally, one of the most important philosophies we can have about meetings is an understanding of the need for compromise. In spite of the fact that compromise sounds like a weakness, it is a way of life. As we will see in Chapter 14, where we talk about negotiating agreements, there is some skill to be learned in knowing how to effect a successful compromise. We recommend that you review that chapter before going into a decision-making or problem-solving meeting. While it might be possible, theoretically, for everyone to have complete agreement on a particular action or idea or solution, in reality it virtually never happens. If we have a philosophy which says that we understand that there will be some compromise taking place, we can go in with our necessities identified and perhaps even with a list of those things we are willing to give up.

PREPARATION

As we begin to prepare for a meeting, we need to ask ourselves a basic question: "Why are we having this meeting at this time with these people?" If we can't find the answer to this question, we would be better off not to have this meeting. If we are satisfied with the answer and all the reasons are legitimate, we can be confident that we're going to have a good meeting. So the first thing to do is make a decision about why

Preparing for a Successful Meeting

To prepare for a successful meeting, technical managers should:

1. Determine the purpose of the meeting
2. Prepare themselves (mentally and physically)

we're having this meeting. One way of doing this is to ask ourselves what would happen if we didn't have this meeting at this time. If the answer to that is "nothing serious," there's a good chance that we don't need the meeting. We've already mentioned the alternative of sending out a memorandum or policy statement, and we might also consider some telephone calls in lieu of having the meeting. Since meetings use up a lot of time and since people don't have time to spare, we need to be careful in having a meeting just for the sake of having one. In fact, if we can, we ought to try very hard to avoid the meeting.

Before we begin preparing for the meeting, we need to decide why we are having it. Once we've made that decision, all of our planning will go in that direction. In the introduction, we mentioned a number of reasons why we have technical meetings. Now let's go back and examine them in more detail.

INFORM OR REPORT

Some meetings simply provide an opportunity to report various activities or progress to members of bigger committees, or to higher management or perhaps to other departments or units. It's not a problem-solving meeting, but merely one to let everyone know where the committee stands on the action they were assigned to do. In preparation for this kind of meeting, we want to be sure we have backup data that explains where we are at this point and how we got there. We certainly should have the information necessary to report the committee's findings so far, and it's probably a good idea to have the support information, too. If it is possible, it's a good idea to send copies of all the information we are going to be using to the people who will be attending the committee meeting. We don't necessarily have to send great volumes of backup data, but it will help to send anything we have that makes a statement about our findings, any conclusion we've reached, or any summary we've made. Of course, we'll want to have that information present at the meeting itself in case there are others who show up or the people forget to bring what we sent them. As we'll see in most of the different kinds of meetings we'll conduct, it is a good idea to call some people ahead of time, especially if they are going to present a certain portion of the information or are going to make a report. At this time, we can tell them how much time we expect to have or specific points or key items we hope to cover; we can then offer to help prepare the material to hand out.

When we are there just to report or inform people about certain things it is good to have some summary graphics. We can take these in the form of projected visual material for letting everybody see quickly what is happening and what has happened previously. These same summaries, charts, or graphs should be duplicated (letter size) to hand out so that people don't have to take notes in the meeting.

PERSUADE OR SELL

There are times when a technical decision has come about as a result of considerable research or exploration or examination of a problem. The decision has been made, but there may be a need for others to get involved. It may be that there are those who need to approve the funds or supply people for further work on the project. It may be that this is going to require time from other departments or units. We might be looking for support or trying to find out if there is support for the decision. In this particular kind of meeting we are either trying to persuade the people to accept the ideas that we have come up with or to sell our idea to them.

There is some advanced preparation needed for this kind of meeting. First, in order to show that our decision is valid, we need to have information that shows the approach we took in arriving at this decision. We may want to have a summary of the alternatives we've considered and the reasons why we chose the particular solution we did. If there are specific people who should be offering support on certain phases of the decision, we would do well to call them in advance and supply them with whatever information they will need in order to speak in favor of the decision. As much as possible, we need to be prepared to point out the ideas or advice that people in the meeting contributed and let them know that their preferences have been considered. As always, in any kind of persuasion or selling situation, we need to be prepared to show the advantages of our decision to the people who are going to be expected to accept it.

ORGANIZE OR RESTRUCTURE

Usually a new project, or an expansion of an older project to a new phase, will call for some kind of meeting to carry out this organization or restructure. The purpose of the meeting would be to set or change the direction. The things that will come out of the meeting will be things like selection of the people to do the future work and assignment of their specific responsibilities. It may be that we will set some timetables, including some specific target dates along the way and checkpoints where we may need additional meetings.

The advance preparation for this is important. We especially want to let everybody know, usually in the announcement of the meeting, what the purpose of this meeting is going to be. We may want to send them a copy of the agenda and a short statement of the decisions that are going to be made at this meeting. Again, we'll want to notify specific people that they are going to be expected to contribute in certain kinds of ways. We will want to make sure that we have the necessary forms available if such are required for organizing or structuring certain activity. Many people find it helpful to have enlarged calendars and handouts for the individual so that any dates and times can be readily seen and recorded. If there is specific backup data or additional information that's going to be needed for the future of the project, we ought to prepare this ahead of time and have it available as handouts.

GET INFORMATION OR IDEAS

Occasionally, committees or groups of people who are working on a specific project come to a dead end or stagnate in their thinking. When this happens, they need to get a fresh look from other people. We can have a meeting of some kind to give the project new life to move on toward completion. It may be that we have just gone as far as we can go with the information that we have and need additional information regarding technical data, money, or budget considerations. We may want to get some opinions on what's been done up to this point. Note that in this kind of meeting we're probably not looking for decisions or approvals; mostly we are looking for hard data, opinions, or suggestions.

In preparation for these meetings we will probably want to send out ahead of time some specific questions we're asking or a summary of the findings so far. We may want to notify certain people by telephone or memo if we expect them to do some preparation ahead of time, look up more information, or bring technical data with them. Certainly we'll want to prepare copies of whatever action or findings we have come to this far in our work. We'll also need some scratch paper or easel paper that so we can write down the suggestions made. It's nearly always a good idea in any kind of meeting to have somebody record the data presented as well as the proceedings we're following.

BRAINSTORMING OR PROBLEM SOLVING

This kind of meeting is similar to the one we just talked about, in which we're trying to get information or ideas. The difference is that this time we are probably looking for solutions, answers to questions, or some specific action we want to take. In the previous meeting, we were getting information or ideas which we can use to solve the problems on our own. In this case, we're giving information and whatever background is necessary, to try to get the people in the meeting to brainstorm a possible solution for us. The goal of this meeting is to come away with specific solutions.

In preparation for this kind of a meeting we're going to have to make sure that we supply backup data in order to keep the people informed about the whole project. We may want to supply at least some summary information ahead of time so that the people can study the material. Again, we want extra copies at the meeting in case they lose their material or forget to bring it with them. We might mention here that we should be very careful in expecting many results to come from advanced preparation by the various members. They will do some amount of reading, but some will also procrastinate or be so busy that they just may not get anything done. If we want specific things done, we should call them by telephone, point out what we want done, get some specific deadlines, and perhaps even follow up on those deadlines to see that the work is done. Again, in preparation we need to make some specific calls to specific people who will be doing some specific things at this technical meeting. When we want people to do something for us that is essential to the success of the meeting, we'll do better to make a personal call rather than just sending a memo. Another thing that we want to do when we are in a brainstorming or problem-solving meeting is to be careful in the selection of our conferees. We should make sure that all the necessary technical expertise is present and that all "factions" or various aspects of the problem are represented. We need to avoid the temptation not to have certain people there who have strong biases, especially if those people are going to have to be committed to the end result of this meeting. We will also want to identify specific outcomes in advance of the meeting. We are not talking about advance solutions, but if there are some necessary conditions that have to be met for the solution, we need to point them out. Finally, the agenda is important so that we will have some kind of barrier to prevent endless debate. Naturally, we have to have some flexibility since we won't know how long the debating or questions are going to last.

MEET REQUIREMENTS

We must admit that sometimes there are organizational or governmental requirements for having certain kinds of meetings at specific intervals or to meet some kind of a law or regulation. Unfortunately these sometimes end up being poor meetings and have a way of turning people against meetings in general. It should not be that way, and it doesn't have to be that way. Actually, these meetings look very much like those meetings we talked about earlier that inform or report. These required meetings may be to satisfy some budget requirement that there be a periodic status report; it may be that we have a periodic meeting on a safety investigation or other investigation that is going on. The meeting may be simply for the purpose of showing that we have, in fact, met certain requirements laid down by the ruling group, whoever that might be.

Even in meetings that are held simply to meet requirements, there is some preparation required. In this case, it may be even more important that we do some advance preparation, because it's a harder meeting to be successful in. First, whatever else we do, we should take the meeting seriously. There are going to be a number of people there who are giving up their production time, and we should do everything we can do to see that they don't waste any more time than necessary. We need a specific agenda, an opening, and a close, and we need to know the specific purpose that this meeting is going to serve. Although we don't want to spend a lot of money if it's not necessary, it's not a bad idea to have some good-looking slides or overheads or other kinds of visuals in order to keep the meeting interesting. We want to make sure to document the actions that are taken in case there are any forms that have to be filled out showing that we have met the requirements. We want to prepare for that ahead of time. We also want to prepare by having someone specifically appointed to record whatever actions are taken in this meeting. If it's necessary to fill out and send forms to someone to show that the meeting has been held, it should be decided ahead of time who is going to do that.

So we see that there is some advance preparation needed

for each kind of meeting that we have. Let's talk for a little bit about building an agenda. The agenda is not necessarily a timetable that's broken down into such small sections that we know at any given moment exactly where we are in that agenda, how long we have, and what the next starting and stopping time is. An agenda is a guideline; it needs to be general enough to allow for flexibility since we aren't always certain what it takes to get agreement or how long it's going to take to get specific information out or across. At the same time, the agenda should be specific enough to keep us from losing control of the meeting or losing control of time. One of the ways of doing this is to list major headings or topics or presentations and allocate a specific amount of time for that particular item. We make that decision by deciding just how much that particular item is worth in terms of the amount of time being put into the meeting. If during the meeting it becomes obvious that we need more or less time than we've allocated, the group rather than the leader can make decisions about this. The group can choose such options as having another meeting to discuss this particular item in more detail, extending the length of this particular meeting with an agreed amount of time to be spent on the subject at hand, or shortening the amount of time that's been allowed for another item with agreement from all the people involved, especially those who might be involved with the item that's losing the time.

Of course, it's possible to have an agenda without having time elements. We can list starting time and optionally list either the specific stopping time or give an approximation as to how long the meeting should last. This has the advantage of a great deal of flexibility, although it loses some of the pressure that time frames give us. People tend to be more relaxed to continue talking even when a decision is made. An agenda that lists times restricts some of the conversation.

If we read the agenda out ahead of time, it becomes a form of a road map that can help sell what we're trying to accom-

Preparing for a Successful Meeting

To prepare for a successful meeting, technical managers should:

3. Build an agenda

plish. This lets the people who dread coming to the meeting know that it is going to be planned, that the time is going to be controlled, and that there is some organization and purpose for this particular meeting.

Although it is not always up to us, we should make some decisions about who attends the meetings. The decision may be made because certain people at certain levels always attend, or because certain people with certain titles or certain responsibilities automatically represent that unit or that division or that department. It may be a political thing; certain people may not want to go if other people of a different level or different department are going to be there. When we make a decision to have people attend who can provide input to the specific decision or problem that we're going to be dealing with, the best rule of thumb is to pick the people who can best discuss the specific topics that are going to be discussed and who can contribute best in whatever function it is we decide that we want them to perform. We should select people on the basis of our need for expertise in the technical matters, their control of money matters, their authority in backing up the decisions that are made, or their ability to represent different technical approaches or viewpoints.

A final thought in preparation is that if at all possible, we should notify people ahead of time to let them know not only that there's going to be a meeting and what's going to be discussed, but also what part they're expected to contribute to

Preparing for a Successful Meeting

To prepare for a successful meeting, technical managers should:

4. Prepare the participants
   a. Notify people ahead of time
   b. Assign roles
5. Prepare the place

the success of this meeting. They need to know that it is an important meeting and that they're an important part of the meeting. They need to know that it is their meeting and that they'll be expected to participate and contribute and to support the findings of the meeting. One of the best ways of doing this is to make a personal telephone call to those people who are going to contribute the most significant parts to the meeting to let them know what your expectations are. If we cannot make a telephone call, we should send them a personal memo—perhaps even handwritten with a copy of the agenda and a positive note about what we want to accomplish through them.

BEGINNING THE MEETING

The meeting should begin with some kind of simple welcome. Ideally we should be there ahead of time in order to prepare the room and take care of the creature comforts, such as a water pitcher or some kind of refreshments if that is a part of the program. If we're there early, we can greet people as they come in and go over with the key people the contributions they are to make. As we prepare the room, we want to make sure that we can find where the lights turn on and off, where the controls for heating and air conditioning are, where the rest rooms are, and where the nearest telephone is. We should try to make arrangements for telephone messages to be taken but left at some place that does not disturb the meeting. We want to see that the necessary visual aids are available and working. We should make sure we have the key people placed where they can be seen or heard if they are going to be using visual aids. We should greet the people coming in informally but still with a businesslike attitude. Even though we've covered it in a memo or telephone call, we may want to get with our key people as they come in to make sure that they have the signals straight and know for sure when they come in and how long they will speak. When the people are seated, the most important thing we can then do is make sure we're on time. Even if some of the people are not there yet, we shouldn't punish those who were there on time by making them wait for the latecomers. The only exception to this is when some of our key people have not yet shown up. Even in this case we should wait only a short time before we begin. We are going to expect to end on time, and the only way we can do this is to start on time.

In our formal welcome to the group we'll need to take care of some housekeeping items. We need to go over the time frame that has been set, making sure that everyone knows when we are going to start or when we'll take a break for refreshments or lunch. We need to establish again the purpose for the meeting, look at the agenda, and establish the procedure we are going to follow. If we are going to have everyone contribute first before there is any discussion, we need to establish that. If we are going to pick one topic or person at a time and discuss some things, we ought to know that ahead of time and establish that with the group. Another part of our welcome is to introduce everyone we can; either go around the room and introduce the people, or have them introduce themselves. Of course if they are familiar with each other, introductions will not be necessary. However, if there is even one person in the meeting who does not know the others, it's not enough to introduce that person. The newcomer has a right to know who the other people are and what their jobs and responsibilities are. If we introduce the people ourselves, we want to be sure to get their names and their job responsibilities right. If they introduce themselves, we need to set the example for them by briefly introducing ourselves, giving our name and job responsibility. One thing is certain; we should make sure that everyone knows not only the people and their job responsibilities but also, as much as we can, the functions that each person will play in this meeting. Finally, we will want to start in a businesslike manner. This sets the precedent for the rest of the meeting. If we start off in a haphazard manner, obviously ill-prepared, or using a lot of humor or jokes, we are setting the tone for how everyone else will act for the rest of the meeting. It's all right to be humorous and it's all right to be relaxed, but we still want to start in a businesslike manner because we are using businesspeople's time. If there are ten people there and they are there for only an hour, that's more than one person-day that we've used in this hour.

USE THE PARTICIPANTS

We've already talked about making it everybody's meeting, not just our own. One of the most successful ways to conduct the meeting is to get different people to play different roles as needed. There are a number of leadership roles that we can share with others. The roles have to be played by somebody, and too often the leader plays all of them. Let's look at some of these and see how they contribute to the success of the meeting.

Conducting a Successful Meeting

To conduct a successful meeting, technical managers should:

1. Begin in a positive, businesslike manner
2. Use the participants

First, we can get some volunteers for some of the specific roles, like a *recorder.* If it's important to take notes of our progress, we might ask someone to volunteer to keep some notes. Of course, if we need extensive recording, we should have someone come in and do that for us so that we will not tie up one of our members. Whenever we assign one of these roles, we want to be sure we do not lose that person as a participant. Once we've gotten someone to agree to be the recorder, we might also ask for a volunteer for a *timekeeper* role. We simply want someone who will let us know when we've spent 30 minutes on a subject or when it's time for a break or when it's necessary to stretch after 45 minutes or whatever time frame we want to set up for the meeting. The role of the timekeeper is to keep us posted as far as time is concerned. Another role that we will need, although we can't ask for volunteers, is the role of the *conscience.* At some point somebody in the group will raise a question as to whether we are really attacking the right problem or whether we are applying ourselves as we ought to. When this happens, we have someone playing the leadership role that we call the conscience. In most of the meetings we go to, this role is played by the leader. The problem with this is that it tends to make the leader the "heavy." He or she appears to be punishing the group for not doing what they're supposed to do. It works much better if someone else in the group plays that role. When someone shows that he or she has an interest in being the conscience by raising the kind of questions we've talked about, we might carry it a step further and say something like, "You know I'm really glad you raised that question, and I appreciate somebody serving as our conscience. How about letting us know when you think we're off the subject or spending too much time on nonproblem-solving activities." From now on we have that person serving in the capacity, and this removes that very heavy role from our responsibilities.

Most of the other roles we look for can't be assigned and may be played by different people at different times. They need to be there, and the leader needs to use them as much as possible. For example, there is the *compromiser* role. Some people are just very good at recognizing the fact that there is a way to bring together two people who appear to be at odds. Whenever anyone in the group tries to serve as a compromiser, we ought to encourage that as much as possible. These are people who are listening to what two or three people are saying, recognizing their differences, and thinking it through to a point that says: "Here is a way that all of you might come to an agreement." If they are successful, they've done you a great favor; even if they are not successful, they give you some grounds to work with and we might follow up on this ourselves.

Another role that is similar to this is the role of the *harmonizer.* The harmonizer is the one who helps keep the peace. He or she is not necessarily the same as the compromiser, but one who looks for opportunities to settle differences between people with positive approaches. The harmonizer brings out the positive statements that different people make and builds on those. This is a very valuable part of the meeting structure; and if someone doesn't play that role, we'll have to ourselves. Another role is that of *devil's advocate.* We really don't like it when people disagree with us, especially in a meeting where we are fighting a time frame and need everybody to agree on something. If we have some there who are honestly raising questions, testing ideas, and making certain that we've examined all elements of the questions, we need to be glad they are there. These people are asking for definition of words, feeding words back to us that we have said, and bringing up the other side of a lot of questions; we need to be careful not to punish these people. At the same time, if these people serve only to block the road and never allow us to go on, we may have to deal with them differently. We may have to get the group to deal with them by turning the questions over to the group with some kind of a statement like, "How do you feel about that?" Anytime the person who seems to be playing the role of devil's advocate says anything that is positive or supportive, we want to make sure that we reward and reinforce this so that he or she will continue to be a member of the team.

Another role that we look for is the role of the *summarizer*. The summarizer is one who keeps us up to date as to where we have come so far and what kind of progress we are making toward specific goals. If we find one or two people who seem to be playing this role, we want to encourage and support them as much as possible in the activity. At some point we may even make it semiofficial by calling on them to serve this function. They may even go to the easel or chalkboard and give other reactions to our progress.

One word of caution, however, is that it is always a dangerous thing to have someone in the meeting get control of the front of the room or the easel or chalkboard. They get a deal of stature by being up front and writing things. If we make a poor choice, they may in fact write down only the things they want to write down and can begin to run the meeting on their own. Of course, as long as the meeting is going where we want it to go, it doesn't really matter who is running it.

HIDDEN AGENDA

Everyone comes to a meeting with some kind of hidden agenda. This is simply a bias against or for certain directions.

It may be something that's left over from a previous meeting or something that's happened on the job. It may be some restriction or some direction that the person's boss has given. The boss may have said, "Be sure you don't agree to this" or "Do your best to get the group to agree on such and such." The hidden agenda may be that they have another engagement after this and they want to get out early. This may cause them to hurry to decisions, make fast agreements, or even withdraw their own participation.

We need to watch for hidden agendas which may or may not be in spoken form. It may be that certain participants seem to have been turned off by something that was said, and they simply withdraw. It may be that they constantly come back to a particular subject and seem to want to talk only about that. It may be that certain people keep getting off the subject as though they are trying to avoid any action. Others may be talking a subject to death without allowing the group to take any kind of specific action. This doesn't necessarily mean that they have a hidden agenda, but it certainly is an indication that they are not completely oriented to action and decision.

When we suspect that certain people are letting their hidden agendas interfere with the progress of the meeting, we may want to take some steps to let them speak out or get their grievances heard. It may be that we can simply say, "I have a feeling that you still have some problem with the decision we are about to make" or "We haven't heard from you about this yet. How do you feel about what we're saying?" Even if this

Conducting a Successful Meeting

To conduct a successful meeting, technical managers should:

3. Watch for hidden agendas

does not get rid of their hidden agenda, you will at least eliminate any excuse they might have for saying later that they did not get to participate.

We may have to remember that we also have hidden agendas and that we have some strong biases that are getting in the way of our conducting the meeting properly. We may have already decided how we want this problem to be solved or exactly what action we want the group to take. If this is true, we need to ask ourselves if we are being open-minded about this or if we are trying to shove something down the throats of the participants. No matter how subtle we may be, the group will finally realize that we are letting our biases get in the way. They will probably say something like, "The leader has already figured out what we're supposed to do. Why are we wasting all this time?"

CONCLUDING THE MEETING

As time begins to run out, we need to think about closing the meeting. The ideal situation is for our meeting activity to run out so that we can conclude the meeting rather than letting time regulate the close of the meeting when we're not yet through with the activities. There is certainly nothing wrong with concluding a meeting before the specified time *if* we have accomplished all that we wanted to accomplish. We certainly should strive to close the meeting at the designated time. This will encourage people to attend additional meetings and build confidence in us as a meeting leader.

Before the meeting is over there is some action we have to take. We've talked about summarizing. Whether we do it ourselves or let another person do it, someone should summarize the actions we have taken, the decisions we have made, and our total outcome. We should establish clearly what the action steps are going to be after we leave this meeting. We want to be sure that we have specified the person or persons who are going to do the particular things decided on and that they know what the standards are for their action. We certainly want to let them know what the deadline is for accomplishing the action steps we have agreed on.

One significant thing that we sometimes forget to do is to get verbal commitment from the entire group on the results of that meeting. It's a good idea to get people committed as much as possible, and one way of doing that is to get them to speak out in favor of what we are going to do. We can do this by asking questions like, "How do you feel about this?" or "Does anyone have a good feeling about the action we are getting ready to take?" This verbal commitment is going to carry over into the workplace; and if there is some selling to be done, we've got a pretty good sales force in the members at this meeting.

Before they leave, we should also make an effort to establish a time for the next meeting, if there is going to be one. It may be that there is some uncertainty as to whether we will even have another meeting or whether everyone can be there. In this case we set a tentative date and make notes of those people who have some conflict. At a later date we can follow up on this in a private way. Once we've established the time for the next meeting, we want to be sure to thank the group for their participation and to say something very positive about the results.

FOLLOW UP

Our job is not finished when the meeting is over. One of the first things we should do if possible, even the same day, is to review our own personal action in the meeting. We need to

Conducting a Successful Meeting

To conduct a successful meeting, technical managers should:

4. Prepare a strong close
5. Follow up

make some mental calculations as to how well we prepared for it, how well we communicated with the people who were there, how well prepared they were when they got there, and how well we did in sharing the leadership roles. We might even make some notes about who played each role best so that we can play on this the next time we have a meeting.

Next, we want to summarize everything that's been said concisely enough that we can make some limited notes and send copies of these minutes to the participants. Here again we'll want to be sure to spell out the specific action we decided to take, who is going to take it, and what the deadlines are. If we do send out any information to the participants, it should include a short "thank you" note for their participation.

We're still not through, however; because if there was some action decided on and some deadlines set, we will lose a lot that we gained in this action if we don't follow up. It is a good idea to check on this a little before the deadline rather than wait until the specific time and find out that they still have not done anything or have not completed it. A telephone call will usually suffice. If it's a complicated project prior to the deadline, we might send them an additional copy of the minutes as a reminder of their action and as a way to see if they have any questions.

A final thing we do is to make some notes in preparation for the next meeting. If it's going to be another meeting with this group, we make some notes about difficulties some of them had and some of the hidden agendas they displayed. We might even consider substitutes or alternatives for future meetings of this group. If we are going to run this future meeting, we should build on the successes of the one we just completed and try to avoid whatever mistakes were made.

CONCLUSION

Meetings have a bad reputation. In many cases they deserve whatever bad thing is said about them, but meetings aren't always bad. Good leaders and good participants have good meetings. We find that since there are different reasons for having meetings, each has a different goal and will accomplish different things; however, we prepare and conduct meetings about the same regardless of purpose. We have some things to prepare. First and foremost we have to prepare ourselves; we have to get ourselves physically and mentally ready and brief ourselves on the topics and whatever technical data we need to review. Then we have to prepare the participants. We have to send them whatever backup information they need, we have to assign various activities and roles for them, and we have to let them know what we are trying to accomplish in the meeting. We have to prepare the meeting room and be sure that all the equipment is there and that all the handout material is available. We see that the creature comforts are taken care of, such as heating and air conditioning, comfortable chairs, and easy visibility, and make sure that each participant can see the others. We need to use the participants in the meeting, not only their expertise in the subject matter, but also by sharing the leadership role with them. When the meeting is over and everybody is clear on what action is going to be taken by whom, we need to follow up to make sure that the action is taken by the deadline we have set. Not all meetings are bad things. Very few of them need to be bad. If we are interested in good meetings, we simply have to use the rules we've talked about here.

Reasons for Holding a Meeting

Following are good reasons for conducting meetings:

1. To inform or report
2. To persuade or sell
3. To organize or reconstruct
4. To get information or ideas
5. To brainstorm or solve problems
6. To meet some requirements

Preparing for a Successful Meeting

To prepare for a successful meeting, technical managers should:

1. Determine the purpose of the meeting
2. Prepare themselves (mentally and physically)
3. Build an agenda
4. Prepare the participants
   a. Notify people ahead of time
   b. Assign roles
5. Prepare the place

Conducting a Successful Meeting

To conduct a successful meeting, technical managers should:

1. Begin in a positive, businesslike manner
2. Use the participants
3. Watch for hidden agendas
4. Prepare a strong close
5. Follow up

chapter fourteen

How Can I Negotiate Agreements?

WHAT IS NEGOTIATION?

Engineers and technical people often find themselves in situations in which they have worked up a plan they consider very sound or a recommendation that has good backup data, but find that not everyone is in agreement with this plan or recommendation. This means that they must do some negotiating in order to sell their idea or get the recommendation or plan accepted. Whenever we are dealing with other people whom we want to accept our information, plan, or supporting data, we're going to find ourselves in some kind of a negotiation situation. Basically, negotiation is the art of giving and taking between people. The key words often are "concession" and "compromise." These are frightening words to the typical technical expert who has put together a proposal or plan that is obviously sound, has good supporting data, and will stand almost any test. Nevertheless, it is important to understand that in any of our dealings with our boss, our peers, our subordinates, or our clients, there must be some give and take. In the process we have to recognize that we can't get everything we want without giving up something, but we can do some trading and can know those things that need to be obtained in exchange for the things we have to give up. That's part of the preparation.

PREPARATION

Let's look at some of the qualities of a good negotiator to see what preparation needs to be made before the negotiation actually takes place. First, the good negotiators know what they can give up out of the proposal. It's not that they want to give it up, but they have studied it well enough to know that there are certain parts important to the basic structure of the proposal or plan, and that there are other parts whose absence will not weaken the proposal too badly. Along this same line, good negotiators are able to determine exactly what has to be kept for the integrity of the proposal or recommendation. Good negotiators know that trading is a good way of getting some things and recognize that trading includes giving up some things. The ideal is to give up something that is not going to hurt too badly, will help the other party involved, and will get something back in the trade that's valuable to us. A good negotiator prepares by studying the plan carefully, knowing the facts, knowing the supporting data, being familiar enough to recognize what will happen if certain things are given up, and knowing what a good trade will do for us. The preparation of a good negotiator also includes learning some things about the other party involved. It may mean talking to some other people to find out something about the person's personality, likes and dislikes, and what the person feels is extremely important and less important. If possible, it's important to know things that are apt to irritate or things that please the person. A final part of the preparation includes taking a look at ourselves to see if there are some areas where we tend to be weak. We need to see if there is something about our personality that is irritating, and whether or not we are too threatened by confrontation and conflict. Knowing ourselves is just as important as knowing the people we are negotiating with.

DURING THE NEGOTIATING PROCESS

Once we have done the proper preparation, it is equally important to have a good negotiation process. By this time we should be prepared and have our confidence up; we should go into the negotiating activity expecting to be successful. A good agenda is the most obvious thing we need as we go into the negotiating meeting. We may have to share this with the person we are negotiating with and come to some kind of an agreement; or we may just have a personal agenda that we can follow. It should include some time frames, what questions need to be settled first, how we are going to make the presentation, when we are going to open the negotiating up for questions and answers, and when the meeting should be over. As silly as that may sound, sometimes we have done a good job of negotiating but fail to realize that the negotiating should be stopped at this point because we have what we want, we've not given up too much and the other party is as satisfied as we are, and it's time to quit.

Another thing that we need to have as we go into this meeting is an objective. We need to know exactly what it is that we are going to be satisfied with; as we've already said, we need to know what we need to keep and what we need to give up. We should have a clear statement in our own mind or on paper as to the minimum we'll be willing to settle for in this nego-

Negotiating Principles

To negotiate successfully, technical managers should:

1. Know what to keep and what to give up
2. Know the other person
3. Understand the situation they're going into, facts, figures, and so on

tiating effort. Ideally, when we begin negotiating, we will want to maintain control. We will want to keep things going, and as much as possible, we will try to keep control of the meeting rather than lose control of it.

One of the very critical ingredients of the whole negotiating process is to try to use the personalities involved, both ours and the people we are negotiating with, as a means of working in a positive way rather than in a negative way. This means finding places where we can agree on issues. We need to let the people know that we want to be fair in our negotiations and that we are not going to be single-minded or stubborn or close-minded about it. It's especially important to get agreement on some of the easier issues fairly early in the negotiation. This will help get the personalities working together and create a harmonious atmosphere when the negotiation gets more difficult later.

Let's just mention a few of the things that happen during the negotiation operation. First, we may want to make our presentation, but not necessarily do an overwhelming job through showing all the facts and figures in supporting data. Keep these in reserve to use when questions begin to be asked. It's always a good idea to sell our point of view by showing the other person the advantages in what we have proposed. We need to be crisp in answering questions, and we need to ask

Negotiating Principles

To negotiate successfully, technical managers should:

4. Use the personalities involved in a positive way

good questions ourselves. The trick of asking good questions is not to put the person on the defensive but to ask a question that is reasonable and not obviously intended to trap the person. *Ask for information, not emotions.* Ask for facts and figures that will contribute to the negotiations rather than just support our position. As the negotiation proceeds, we want to be sure not to feel that we have to answer every objection immediately or that we have to make a decision. Rather, we need to catalog the things that are being said so that we can use them as trade-offs as we begin the matter of making concessions or compromising, which is the heart of the negotiation.

As we progress we are going to have to handle certain objections that arise. As people start to raise questions and indicate that they don't like a particular part, rather than getting defensive or emotional we take a very positive approach, show the backup data as though there is no question about it, and ask for suggestions for a better way of doing it. We need to remember that we have to put a lot of time into this, that we really know what we are talking about, and that we should be able to overcome the objections that people have. But there are small issues that arise which we see we can give up. We can make statements like, "Well, I hadn't thought all that much about not using that; but if we did that, would it be possible for you to go ahead and define what we are looking for?" Simple rule: never voluntarily give up something without asking for something in return. Answer questions and deal with questions before they get to be too large or before too much conflict arises. At the same time, when we do get an answer from somebody, we may want to make sure that the person really means it, is willing to stand behind it, and can support that answer. There may be some hidden agendas in the person's mind. As we gradually sell our ideas and begin to see that the negotiation is going to be successful, we need to start thinking about the future. We should be sure that the person doing the negotiating has the final say so. If not, we need to find out very quickly who can give us an answer, and we need to get this in writing. Ask for a specific deadline and assume openly that all of this is going to take place. Perhaps the worst thing we can do is negotiate long and diligently and come out in good shape, only to find out that the person we dealt with doesn't really have the authority to make the decision. There are going to be times when for one reason or another our ideas are not bought. We need not think of it as something that's very personal and feel very bad about it. We just simply have to learn from this and do a better job of negotiating the next time.

AFTER THE NEGOTIATION

However the negotiation comes out, if we're still going through with the proposal, it is important to get some kind of a memorandum of agreement as soon as possible. It is a good idea to have notes of the minutes or notes of the agreements handwritten and have copies given to each person. If not, we should take the step of writing memorandums, spelling out the specific actions on the part of each person, and listing the action items as they were agreed on. We should sign the memorandum and send it to the people concerned. Don't have additional negotiating words, such as "If you have prob-

Negotiating Principles

To negotiate successfully, technical managers should:

5. Get some kind of agreement as soon as possible

lems with this let me know" or "If this is not in accordance with your thinking, I'd appreciate hearing from you." Put a positive statement in the memorandum that says, "This is the agreement as I recall it, and I wanted to make sure that you had a copy of it as quickly as possible."

The more we negotiate, the better we are going to be at it. We can learn from our poor negotiating, and we can get very good at it if we are not only well prepared and able to support our material, but also approach the whole thing with a very positive, confident, professional air.

We have noted some things about negotiations, including the beginning and ending as well as the actual negotiation. Now let's see how these things can be put into practice. We are going to look at two or three different ways of handling the same problem and comment on each. The situation is this: Fred Summers is the supervisor of project management in engineering. He has working for him a number of people, including Joe Corley. Joe has a considerable amount of service and is a senior to some of the other people. He is going to be in charge of an important project. It's going to be necessary for Fred to change Joe's seating to another location which will appear to have less prestige. The office is long and narrow and Fred has a private room halfway between the engineers on one side and the clerical people on the other. At the engineering end, desks are lined up each side of the wall without any partition between them. It's generally considered that it is more prestigious to be farther away from the center. As new people come in to replace those who are leaving, the system has been for senior people to take the seats toward the end.

Joe Corley is about two thirds of the way down in a room of some ten engineers. The work flow is changing to the extent that it is now important to have Joe very close to Fred's office, especially for the next year. Joe is going to be riding herd over a project that is to begin shortly, and there will often be times when people from other groups will be coming in. They will need to meet in Fred's office and Joe will need to be in most of these meetings. Also, because of the importance of the project, Fred will be attending a number of meetings at other locations and will need a quick briefing from Joe. This is going to require clerical support, and being close to the center will allow Joe to have access to a drafting clerk who will be assigned to him at all times and other clerical support as he needs it. The question is: How is Fred going to make this work and not upset the balance of prestige in the office or cause Joe to have some loss of face? There are several choices that Fred, as the boss, has in handling this situation. Let's note some of them:

1. Because he is the boss, Fred can simply tell Joe that this is his decision, and Joe will have no choice but to comply.
2. Fred can try to sell Joe on the idea by argument or pressure or selling.
3. Fred can try to get Joe to think it's his own idea and make it appear that there are several options.
4. Fred could explain what he wants and negotiate with Joe, if there are negotiations.

Let's examine these and see how each might work. We'll let Fred try one or two of them and see what kind of results he gets. First, there is the matter of Fred being the boss and simply telling Joe of his decision. We don't have to see how this would go because it would work very well from the standpoint of there not being any argument. Of course, the after effects are that Joe will feel that he had no say in the matter. He will perceive himself as having lost face with the rest of the people and will feel that his prestige is less. Altogether, he will never be happy in the new arrangement and he will not be able to give as much support to the project as perhaps he should. Also, he's got to answer to the other engineers at break time and lunchtime as they either kid him or ask him why he's had to move. This is not to say that there are not times when we would need to use this approach, but this doesn't seem to be the best place to use it.

Let's see what would happen if Fred uses the second idea of argument or pressure or selling.

Fred: Come on in, Joe. I would like to talk to you about this new project we're undertaking.

Joe: Sure, I'm glad I'm going to be involved in it. Sounds like it's going to be a good-sized project, one that we'll all learn some things from, and I think I'll have some fun.

Fred: I'm sure you will, and the sooner we get started the better. What I had in mind was that we need to do some changing here, and I've decided that it would work out a lot better if you were sitting closer to me so that I could have access to you and to your files.

Joe: What do you mean, *closer*?

Fred: Oh, I had in mind that we could change things around so that you could have the desk that adjoins my office.

Joe: Well, that's not the choicest spot in the office. The lighting is not all that good, and usually that's the seat that the beginners take.

Fred: Yes, I know that, but I think that we're all mature enough not to worry about those kinds of things. This is an important project, and everybody knows that you've been around for a while and certainly you aren't worried about things like prestige and how all of this will look to the rest of the people.

Joe: Well, I am not so sure that I'm not worried about some of these things. I've been here several years, and I like where I am and there is good lighting—it's close to the window, the heating and air conditioning both seem to be very good, and it's a lot quieter.

Fred: I hope we're not going to make a big issue out of this. I just figured I could count on you since you're one of the most understanding engineers we have. I didn't think we would have to go through any big deal just to get some desks changed.

This is enough to see that all of this is going to lead to an unhappy Joe. Actually, it's not much different from the first method. It's obvious that Fred's made up his mind and that Joe is going to be expected to take this. There was some pressure there along with a little effort to do some selling. There was a feeble attempt to flatter Joe, but mostly Fred told him he knew he wasn't going to act the way that he was indeed acting. It wasn't a very good effort on Fred's part, and we would assume that he really wouldn't use it any more than he would use the first one.

Let's look at the third option that Fred has in making the arrangements for moving the engineers. In this case we are going to see Fred try to convince Joe it was his idea and to make it appear that there were some options open and at this point there were no final decisions. Let's see how that conversation might go.

Fred: Joe, I thought maybe we might want to talk about this new project.

Joe: Well, I sure would like to. I'm excited about it. I'm glad we are getting into it, and I'm glad we got the project. I hope I'll be able to handle it.

Fred: I'm sure not worried about that, Joe. If anyone can handle it, I'm sure you can. With the experience you have and the knowledge you have on this subject it won't be too big a task for you.

Joe: Well, I appreciate your confidence, and I'm sure I'll have a lot of questions along the way; but I'll give it everything I've got.

Fred: I'm sure you will, that's why you've got this assignment. There is something I want to talk about, though, before we get you started.

Joe: Oh, what's that?

Fred: Well, for one thing, maybe it's a good idea to consider some changes in our desk locations.

Joe: What did you have in mind?

Fred: Actually, I just thought I'd talk to you about it and see how you felt. I was thinking that we're going to be work together a lot, and maybe it would work out a little better if we were closer together.

Joe: You mean I should move my desk somewhere else, closer to you?

Fred: Well, what do you think about that? I was just making some suggestions, thinking out loud.

Joe: I don't know that it's all that complicated for me to travel from where I am to where you are. I don't know how much we'll be doing together; you know much more about that than I do.

Fred: Well, you'll also be working with the drafting clerk and our other support people. What do you think about being close to them?

Joe: It looks to me like we're talking about only a few feet, and I don't know that a few more steps are going to wear me out.

Fred: Well, there are going to be times that I'm going to have meetings in my office and people will be coming in; some will want to see me and some will want to see both of us together.

Joe: Well, just let me know, and I'll be glad to talk to them.

Fred: It'll be a little awkward for you way back in the room to have people coming in there to talk to you.

Joe: I don't mind that.

Fred: Well, there will be times when I will need you to brief me pretty quickly because I may get a call from Bill Morris my boss. If you were closer to my office, you could come in even while I was on the telephone with him in case he had any immediate problems.

Joe: If that's what you want me to do, I'll do it; but I don't see that it's such a big problem. I like where I am.

We can see that Fred is pretty much back in the same situation as the first and second methods produced. If he's going to get Joe to move using this approach, he's going to have to tell him. Joe doesn't want to move. He likes where he is; and no matter how good the arguments are, it's going to be hard to convince him. Notice that in none of the three situations we have talked about so far has there been any negotiation. There hasn't even seemed to be any room for any negotiation. Fred has not offered any options; Joe has not sought any. This brings us to the fourth choice that Fred has in dealing with this problem. If he goes through the steps we've talked about already, he will be well aware that Joe doesn't want to move, that there is some prestige involved, and that there will have to be some trading. He knows some things about the project, and he knows the plan he has in mind. He doesn't have a whole lot of time to debate the issue, but he would like for Joe to be satisfied with the final decision. This brings Fred to the position of whether or not he has anything to trade. Let's look at another dialogue between the two and see if Fred does a good job of negotiating.

Fred: Come in, Joe. I wanted to talk to you about the new project and some ideas I had about setting up the work flow.

Joe: That's good. I'm excited about it, and I hope I can do as good a job as you want me to on this new project.

Fred: Well, I wouldn't have picked you if I hadn't believed that you could do it. You've got all the experience and background we need, and you'll be able to work with the other people following this project through for the next year without much trouble.

Joe: I appreciate your confidence. I'm sure there will be times when I'll need to call on you for some help.

Fred: You call on me anytime you want to, Joe. I'll do my best to keep other people out of the way and make the necessary arrangements for you to talk to whomever you need to.

Joe: Well, I appreciate that. How are we going to get started on it?

Fred: Well, let me tell you what I have in mind. As I've been looking at the work flow, it seems that you and I are going to spend a lot of time together for the next year. Also, you are going to have to spend some time with the clerical people; and as you know, we've assigned you a full-time drafting clerk.

Joe: Sure can't argue with that. I don't know what you have in mind as far as our spending time together, but I'm sure there will be questions that I'll have.

Fred: There will be more than questions, Joe. We'll be having a lot of meetings, and we'll have people coming in from the other groups, especially at the very beginning. Toward the end of the project we'll have meetings. It would not surprise me that for the first month we'll have one or two meetings a day. After that we'll certainly have weekly meetings, and there will be other people involved periodically.

Joe: Wow, I didn't realize we'd be spending that much time in meetings.

Fred: Well, they won't be long meetings, but we'll need to get together quickly sometimes. There is also the matter that you will need to brief me when I'm talking to my boss, Bill Morris. He will also have some meetings at the beginning and near the end, and he will want some progress reports. That means that I need to have access to you even while he's still on the phone so that I can meet his needs.

Joe: Well, what did you have in mind? Were you talking about me moving?

Fred: Well, based on what we've said, the most obvious thing is for you to take the desk right outside my office. That will give you access to the clerical and support people and give them access to you without going down and disturbing the other engineers. It would also give you access to me when you need to ask questions. You can use my office to meet in when you have people coming in from the outside. Obviously we are going to have to move fast when my boss wants some information and has some people in his office or on the telephone.

Joe: Well, I'm sure you recognize that I've been here a pretty good while, and I like where I am. It's taken me a while to get there.

Fred: I recognize that, and I knew that when I called you in. I can also see where it would be a matter of some prestige to be where you are, and I'm sure the lighting is better.

Joe: That's true; so is the temperature. The temperature is not very even in this room, and it seems like where I am now is the best choice of heating and air conditioning.

Fred: We can get the engineering people in here who handle the air conditioning and heating to change the vent flow if necessary.

Joe: Well, that would certainly have to be done if I moved up closer, but I guess you know that's the place we've always thought of as being the new engineer's location, and I don't know what the other people will think.

Fred: Well, what would it take to change their minds? Certainly they know that this is a special project, and I'll be glad to call them in and talk to them about this new arrangement.

Joe: Well, that might not be a bad idea since they're going to be seeing people coming and going, and some will probably think about asking me questions on their own projects.

Fred: It's not my idea that you'll be working on any other project, and I'd rather you not be disturbed.

Joe: Would it be possible to have that said to them so they'd know that I'm not available when they want help?

Fred: Sure, I'll be glad to tell them that. As a matter of fact, I'll just simply tell them that if they have some problems to come to me; and if I think it is important enough or urgent enough, I'll call you in and let you make the decision as to whether you want to take time off to help them.

Joe: Well, if I did move, I wonder if it would be possible to build a temporary closed-in office so that I could have the meetings in my space.

Fred: Well, since we're talking about a year's project, I can see where having some privacy is going to pay off; but this is not a secret project and we certainly wouldn't have to build a closed-in office.

Joe: I was just thinking that it might disturb the other people if I were in the bull pen like it is now and had two or three people sitting around my desk talking.

Fred: Well, I'll tell you what I can do. I think we can afford to rent some movable partitions and put them up beside your desk and credenza, and that way you'd be isolated from them and yet we wouldn't have set a precedence to build a private office.

Joe: That would give me some places to put some charts on the wall, and also allow me to have the meetings if I wanted them.

Fred: I think that's a good idea, and we could take care of that right away. One of the things I would want you to agree on, of course, is that when this project is over you wouldn't object to moving back to the place you are now.

Joe: Well, I think that's to be expected, and I'll have no problem with that. Would it be possible for me to have the drafting clerk move her desk right opposite me?

Fred: Well, I think that would confuse things somewhat because she needs access to the supplies that are in their offices, and it might be a little awkward to have meetings with her sitting right outside your door. I'll tell you what we might do, though. We've already got a telephone system that will allow us an intercom, and I'll work up an arrangement where you can buzz her or she can buzz you and you can talk on the intercom.

Joe: That sounds like a good idea. It'll give me access to her when I need her, and she could ask me questions if she wanted to.

Fred: I think that's a good idea, and I'll have it set up so I can buzz you if I need you.

Joe: That's good; then I can come when you've been talking to someone, or you need a question answered right away.

We see that when Fred began to do some negotiating, he was very skilled at it. He did have some things to trade, and in the negotiating he got what he wanted. He gave up some things that were not too significant. He did make some concessions. There were times when he countered a request by Joe with a trade-off, offering him something different but solving the same problem. He also got commitments from Joe. It was interesting that in the beginning the question was, "How can we get Joe to move to this less-than-prestigious position?" and before it was over, we got Joe to the location where he is now. That was good negotiating. What were some of the trade-offs? Joe wanted a full-time private office; Fred offered to rent a partition. Joe wanted the drafting clerk to sit opposite his desk; Fred offered to install an intercom arrangement. Fred wanted and got a commitment from Joe to move back to the other location when the assignment was over. This helped to build the prestige of this new location and make it appear a desirable one. Joe wanted Fred to tell all the other people he could not help them on their projects; Fred offered a compromise. He offered to tell them the importance of this project and that if they had any need for Joe's help, they could come to him and he would decide whether or not Joe should help on the project. In other words, he did not lose Joe's help nor the decision to get Joe to help if it was important, but he satisfied Joe in the process.

Thus we see that it is possible to put these negotiating principles into practice. What we've seen is that some of the key words in negotiation are *trade, compromise, concession.* It's funny, but those words somehow imply a tint of weakness. *Trading* sounds like selling cars; *compromise* sounds like we're giving in, as does *concession.* In reality, as we have seen, we don't necessarily have to give up something significant when we trade. A compromise may mean that what we're getting is better than what we're giving up. The concession that we make is simply a means of getting something that is important and leaving the people we're negotiating with satisfied that they do not lose face or have to give up too much.

CONCLUSION

Negotiating is an admirable profession. If we do our work ahead of time by understanding the person or persons with whom we're negotiating and understanding the situation we're going into, including the facts and figures about the thing we're negotiating, and if we are aware all the time during

Negotiating Principles

To negotiate successfully, technical managers should:

1. Know what to keep and what to give up
2. Know the other person
3. Understand the situation they're going into, facts, figures, and so on
4. Use the personalities involved in a positive way
5. Get some kind of agreement as soon as possible

the negotiating process of what we are getting and giving up, we'll have a great deal of success in our efforts. When the negotiating is over, we also need to follow up to make sure that everything is settled. We have seen that we don't reopen the negotiations but rather state them as facts and past history on which we intend to act and make future decisions. Negotiating can be fun if we do it well, but it can be frustrating if we do it poorly.

chapter fifteen

How Can I Help My Group Handle Special Situations?

INTRODUCTION

Maybe you've said to yourself (as we have): "Just when I learned the answers they changed all the questions!" Time and time again, when we've just managed to get things "under control," some unforeseen event throws them out of control again right before our eyes.

Sometimes the unforeseen event has seemed positive: the gain of a sought-after employee, the promotion of an employee, a major technical breakthrough. Sometimes the unforeseen event has been negative: the loss of funds to a competing project, the transfer of a valued employee, the failure of a project to progress as expected, the death of an employee.

Positive or negative, any change creates imbalance. In a state of imbalance, a work group is likely to revert to an earlier stage of development. It's likely to withdraw energy from the task and redirect it toward status and power issues within the group. And—if the change is negative—if it brings about a perceived loss to members of the group—a reaction much like the grief that follows a friend's death is likely to absorb the group energy.

To illustrate, let's look at the impact of a change in the research and development division. We'll see how Matt Stephens, the division manager, dealt with the reactions of his staff when he announced the promotion of an employee.

Matt announced to the division that Janice Ashford had been selected to manage a new division of the company. She would remain in her job as computer section chief for about three more months. If all went well, her replacement would be selected within four or five weeks so that Janice would have time to "fill him in" before she left.

A less experienced manager would have expected Janice to show unbridled enthusiasm during the coming weeks and the rest of the group to proceed with business as usual. But Matt knew better. He knew he would need to:

Cushion the stress likely to show up in Janice's behavior and in the behavior of other group members.

Accept a temporary setback in team effort. Expect the group to revive old status and power issues and to show more dependence on him.

Help some members of the group as they worked through the stages of grief. Several others had hoped to be selected for the new job. They could experience Janice's good fortune as a significant loss in their careers.

Absorb some of the dissonance as individual reactions to the change unfolded at different rates.

CUSHION THE STRESS

Since we've already dealt with listening skills and their importance, let's just take a quick look at what a technical manager can expect. After her initial excitement over her new

Cushioning Stress Resulting from Changes

To cushion the stress that results from changes in the work situation, technical managers can:

1. Expect it and treat it as a "natural" sequence of events
2. Listen to employees "blow off steam" without reacting adversely

job, Janice seemed subject to wide mood swings. One minute she would seem uncharacteristically effervescent; a minute later she would be cranky or more withdrawn than usual. One minute she would thank Matt warmly for his guidance and support; a short time later she would snap, "I wouldn't be so nervous about handling this new job if you'd delegated to me like you should have all along!" Janice's desk become covered up with junk food. Matt seldom saw her when she wasn't munching on a candy bar or some potato chips.

Fortunately, Janice's mood swings and her junk-food binges didn't take Matt by surprise. He realized that an accumulation of small changes or a few major changes can cause significant stress—even when the changes are positive ones. Thomas Holmes and Richard Rahe conducted a series of studies on stress and health. They concluded that point values could be assigned to specific life changes. (For more information, see Thomas H. Holmes and Richard H. Rahe, 1967.) They believe that a person who accumulates over 150 points in a year has a 37% chance of experiencing physical problems as a result of stress, a person who accumulates over 200 points has a 51% chance, and a person who accumulates over 300 points is facing even greater odds. These positive events are among those on their scale:

Marriage	50 points
Marital reconciliation	45 points

Business readjustment	39 points
Change to a different line of work	36 points
Change in responsibilities at work	29 points
Outstanding personal achievement	28 points
Vacation	13 points
Christmas	12 points

This one positive change in Janice's life could account for 132 "stress points" (business readjustment, change to a different line of work, change in responsibilities at work, outstanding personal achievement). And since some changes in her personal life are likely, Janice certainly experienced enough stress to alter her behavior and perhaps enough to affect her physical health.

Matt's reaction? He simply accepted the mood swings as a natural sequence of events, reminded himself that Janice's behavior was not a personal attack on him, and maintained his usual, steady pattern of behavior as much as possible.

ACCEPT A TEMPORARY SETBACK IN TEAM EFFORT

What could Matt expect? For one thing, he could expect more dependency on him for decisions about what people's assignments were and how Matt wanted them carried out. For another thing, he could expect more conflict over who had authority to do what, about the interpretation of rules and regulations, about the "unwritten rules" that determine appropriate protocol.

Handling a Reduction in Team Effort

To accept a temporary setback in team effort, technical managers can:

1. Expect it
2. Listen
3. Accommodate some overdependent behavior
4. Redirect behavior that is headed through improper channels

So Matt wasn't surprised when his secretary, Joyce, asked the correct procedure for filing a report she had filed on her own for years. He wasn't surprised when Wade (chief of new product development) came in for help in painstakingly completing a budget update—an administrative requirement that he often ignored or completed frivolously. Matt wasn't surprised when Roger, who generally shuns administrative rules and regulations, came into Matt's office with a long list of specific questions about the conditions under which he could grant an employee compensatory time off.

Matt wasn't even surprised when petty conflict flared up. Larry, usually a skillful "people person," accused Roger of "bending the rules to suit yourself." Joyce reacted to a simple request from Shelley by snapping "You're not my boss. You're not supposed to be telling me what to do!"

How did Matt deal with these out-of-character behaviors? To being with, he just listended a lot. After an employee had blown off some steam, if a specific request or demand remained for Matt to deal with, he used one of two strategies. If a request would have been appropriately channeled through Matt by a new employee, Matt accommodated the request even though it was from an experienced employee. If a request would have been inappropriate for even a new employee to channel through Matt, he redirected it.

For example, if Joyce had been a new employee, Matt would have been the person to ask about filing her report. If Wade had been a new employee, Matt would have been the person to ask about compensatory time off. So Matt handled both these requests by providing the minimum amount of information needed to respond.

On the other hand, Shelley and Roger both came to Matt with questions about computer programming. Of course, Matt managed a division that housed a computer section. But computers certainly weren't his specialty. He had long ago decided to delegate those questions to Janice. So he referred Shelley and Roger back to the established channel with a comment like:

> I know there's some confusion in that section now because of Janice's new job. But Janice is still the one to handle that question for you. I think she is in her office now. Why don't you call over there now and ask her if she's free to talk to you?

HELP MEMBERS OF THE GROUP WORK THROUGH THE STAGES OF GRIEF

When Elizabeth Kübler-Ross (1969) studied the terminally ill and their families, she found that they experienced this sequence of emotions: denial, anger, bargaining, depression, and acceptance. Once Kübler-Ross identified this pattern, others noticed it in people's reactions to other kinds of loss: divorce, withdrawal from alcohol abuse, the loss of a dream, the loss of a job, the loss of an opportunity.

Matt knew that several other employees had hoped to be selected for Janice's new job. Some experienced the news of

Helping Group Members Work through Grief

To help members of a group as they work through the stages of grief, technical managers can:

1. Expect employees to go through this sequence in response to a loss: denial, anger, bargaining, depression, acceptance
2. Listen
3. Give employees reassurance of their worth without minimizing their loss
4. Avoid giving advice, telling "war stories," and asking a lot of direct questions

Janice's promotion as a significant loss in their careers. So Matt wasn't surprised at comments characteristic of the stages of grief.

Denial: You've got to be kidding! Surely they didn't give Janice that job. You've just been listening to the wrong grapevine. I'll check with Matt myself to see what's *really* going on.

Anger: There's no such thing as fair treatment around this place. Talk about discrimination! Janice wouldn't have gotten that job if she'd been a man. She's not nearly as suited for it as I am. I've a good mind to walk right out!

Bargaining: Look, I've been around here a long time, and I've done a good job. What are you going to do to make it worth my while now that they've given Janice that prize job?

Depression: I try and try and can't seem to get anywhere. What's the use? I might as well give up.

As with other reactions to the promotion, Matt's most helpful response was simply to listen. And as he did so, he did his best to remember that these emotional reactions were perfectly natural reactions to a loss. They weren't signs of inevitable collapse in his division, they weren't personal attacks directed to him. He knew that he would eventually hear comments signaling that people had worked through the loss.

Acceptance: This has been a real blow. I really believed I would get that job. But now I guess it's time for me to figure out where I'll go from here.

Note: You almost "need to be there" to distinguish acceptance from other stages. It's the tone as much as the words that makes the difference. And the tone is curiously *free* of emotion: free of anger, free of depression, free of happiness.

As his employees worked through their loss, Matt provided reassurance of their worth. He listened, he gave understanding, and—allowing each employee some freedom to set the pace—he used the motivation techniques we mentioned in Chapter 9. For example, to Wade he said:

> That research project you proposed last year has finally gotten some attention in the front office. When you're ready, let's talk about what to do next. I think we have a good crack at it.

Notice that Matt's reassurance in no way minimized Wade's loss. In fact, there were several things that Matt was careful to avoid: giving advice, telling "war stories" (his own tales of woe), and asking a lot of direct questions. In *When bad things happen to good people* (1981, pp. 101–102), Harold Kushner illustrated what harm these things to avoid can do. In Kushner's illustration, Beverly has come to her parents after her husband had walked out on her.

> Stunned, Beverly drove to her parents' home and broke the news to them. They cried with her, comforted her, alternated between bitterness at her husband and practical advice about lawyers, house keys, and bank accounts.
>
> After dinner that evening, Beverly's mother . . . took her aside and tried to talk to her about it. Trying to be helpful, she asked about their sex life, their finances, their patterns of interaction, looking for any clue to what might have caused the problem. Suddenly Beverly threw down her coffee cup and burst out, "Will you please stop this? I'm tired of hearing, 'Maybe if you had done this' and 'Maybe if you hadn't done that.' You make it sound like it was all my fault. You're telling me that if I had tried harder to be a good wife, he wouldn't have left me. Well, that's not fair. I was a good wife. I don't deserve to have this happen. It's not my fault!"
>
> And she was right. . . . It is gratuitous, even cruel, to tell the person who has been hurt . . . "maybe if you had acted differently, things would not have turned out so badly." When we say that, all we are really telling them is, "This is your fault for having chosen as you did. . . ."

ABSORB SOME OF THE DISSONANCE

When Matt announced Janice's promotion, Shelley exploded on the spot. Almost instantly after the event itself, Shelley became acutely aware of its impact on her and exploded into action (or reaction). Before long Shelley had settled back down into the routine of things and was carrying out business as usual.

Roger, on the other hand, seemed almost unaware of the announcement for a long time—even though he had heard it in person just like Shelley. It was a long time before Matt started hearing expressions of anger from Roger. So long, in

Absorbing Individual Reactions to Change

To absorb some of the dissonance as individual reactions to the change unfold at different rates, technical managers can:

1. Expect different reaction rates from different employees
2. Listen

fact, that Roger's behavior seemed out of place. Even other employees who had been upset about Janice's selection seemed to resent that Roger "keeps dragging it out."

When a person has experienced loss, the stages of grief are part of a larger sequence in reaction to an event, as shown in the following diagram. Not only will people move through the stages of grief at different rates, they will also move through the larger sequence at different rates. It simply took Roger a longer time to get to his grief than it did Shelley.

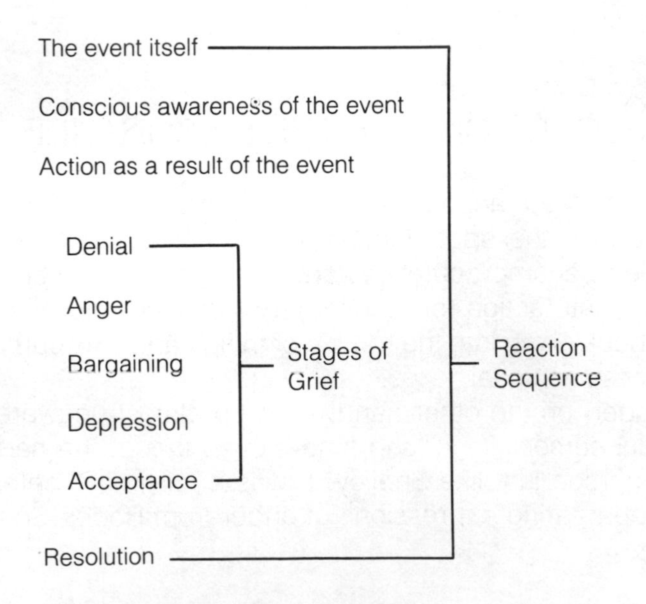

It took longer for an awareness of the impact of Janice's promotion to "sink in."

So Matt needed to deal with employees at different stages in resolving that loss. And he needed to absorb the dissonance caused by behavior that seemed out of place to some. His most helpful response? You guessed it. He listened. Simply listened.

CONCLUSION

Any significant change—positive or negative—will throw a work group into a state of imbalance. The group is likely to revert to an earlier stage of development, to direct its energy once more to power and status issues, to experience a reaction by some employees that is much like grief.

When a change produces these reactions in a work group, technical managers can help if they will

Cushion the stress

Accept a temporary setback in team effort

Help members of the group as they work through the stages of grief

Absorb some of the dissonance as individual reactions to the change unfold at different rates

Cushioning Stress Resulting from Changes

To cushion the stress that results from changes in the work situation, technical managers can:

1. Expect it and treat it as a "natural" sequence of event
2. Listen to employees blow off steam without reacting adversely

Handling a Reduction in Team Effort

To accept a temporary setback in team effort, technical managers can:

1. Expect it
2. Listen
3. Accommodate some overdependent behavior
4. Redirect behavior that is headed through improper channels

Helping Group Members Work through Grief

To help members of a group as they work through the stages of grief, technical managers can:

1. Expect employees to go through this sequence when they've experienced a loss: denial, anger, bargaining, depression, acceptance
2. Listen
3. Give employees reassurance of their worth without minimizing their loss
4. Avoid giving advice, telling "war stories" and asking questions

Absorbing of Individual Reactions to Change

To absorb some of the dissonance as individual reactions to the change unfold at different rates, technical managers can:

1. Expect different reaction rates from different employees
2. Listen

chapter sixteen

How Do I Train Technical and Professional People?

INTRODUCTION

Why do we even consider training technical and professional people, who are already among the best educated and skilled in the organization? Is it not true that they have the background and ability to learn on their own if there is something they are short on? Would it not be better to train those who are less skilled and less educated? While these questions have some obvious answers, they are questions that even highly skilled and educated professional people ask. It may be somewhat of an insult to suggest that they need training; an ego problem may develop if they think they will have to go back to the classroom after all the years they've spent there. But we have some things going for us in the way of motivation or incentives to make the training reasonable and important. The truth is that we don't train everyone because not everyone makes an important enough contribution to utilize the training we give them. Some people have jobs that don't have enough of an impact on the overall outcome of the operation to justify the time, effort, and money spent on training. Since training represents an investment in the future, the implication is clear that we expect the trained people to be with us and contribute to the growth and progress of the organization. However, training isn't intended to meet the ego needs of people or to solve their hang-ups. The idea is to meet the needs of the organization when only training will do that. The basis for any training should fall in one of the following categories:

1. There is something an employee can't do that we want him or her to be able to do, or
2. We want people to do something better than they are now doing it, and we think they have the ability to improve with some training, or
3. People are doing something incorrectly, and we need to change their way of doing it.

OBSOLESCENCE

Typically, there is more obsolescence in most organizations in the technical areas than in any other part of the operation. This has certainly become even more true in more recent years because of the highly complex ways that we are doing things. We're having to play "catch-up" in training and development. We find people who yesterday were at state-of-the art readiness but who today are almost outdated. Add to this the fact that—because of the uniqueness of most technical activities within the average organization—it is a rare thing that technical and professional people can be effective immediately at their hiring point with a company. Put simply: the new people will require training to become effective and the experienced people will require training to stay effective.

UNIQUENESS IN TRAINING AND DEVELOPMENT

We've already seen that technical and professional people have some unique characteristics. The same holds true as far as training and developing them is concerned. One primary consideration is that they need a *reason* for the training. It takes some *time* for them to learn something, and if they are going to take time off the job to learn whatever it is we're teaching, they need to believe that there are some measurable benefits in the learning. Most of the time, they are used to almost "attacking" the learning effort, so there is energy to be expended. They don't mind the effort, nor is there any fear of failure on their part, but they still consider it an imposition if they are asked to expend their time and energy on something they don't perceive as useful or meaningful to them.

Another consideration regarding their uniqueness is that they are less likely to accept a new way of doing things just because "management has decided that this is the way it should be done." When highly technical people find themselves in a situation where they are being asked to learn something that to them makes little or no sense, and the explanation is either, "This is the way management wants it" or "It's not our job to question management decisions," the trainer will have a difficult job.

Technical people are less likely to accept things taught to them by those considered to be less technical or professional or those without legitimate credentials for teaching the subjects at hand. Even if the instructor is experienced in the field—which is almost a "must"—the teacher needs to be respected in the field or be a present practitioner. A nonpractitioner, nonexperienced, nonrespected person trying to instruct a group of highly technical and professional practitioners is in an almost impossible situation.

There is a natural curiosity among most technical and professional people that makes teaching and learning much easier, but sometimes there is more interest in *learning* the new technique or information than there is in *applying* it. Any hope for successful application of the things learned is going to have to come from some need to make the application. Sometimes this is only a matter of letting people discover the advantages of the new data or skill on their own; this will build some commitment on their part.

Another unique fact about this population is that their ability to grasp new concepts and new skills is usually much better than that of less technical employees. They aren't necessarily a smarter group; but they do have a strong background and a very good record of learning. They've rarely had the experience of failing in a learning effort, and they go into any teaching/learning situation with the expectation of succeeding. That mental attitude is often enough to put them in a frame of mind to learn better. The obvious precaution is that they get pretty restless when the training goes at a slow pace, as though they were having trouble absorbing the material. The instruction needs to move at a pace that is challenging. For most, this will keep the learning interesting.

A final consideration in the uniqueness category is one related to several already mentioned. Technical people usually act and react very quickly in a learning environment. They can often see where the instructor is going before a sentence is finished or a conclusion is reached. As soon as they get the gist of the direction, they may outrun the instructor. They also interact well with the written word, hence can handle advanced assignments. These assignments need to have obvious application to their learning goals, of course, and not be perceived of as "busy work."

Although these learners have some unique characteristics compared to nontechnical employees, we also want to discuss some of the things that all learners have in common. There are some considerations that must be taken into account in any learning situation, regardless of the nature of the learner. In this chapter we discuss many of these and their application to the technical development of our more professional employees. There are a number of questions that must be answered before successful training can take place, and we address these next.

DEVELOPING A TRAINING PHILOSOPHY

Question: Does training *really* make a difference?

Answer: This is a question that has to be answered for several groups and entities in the organization.

The *organization* has to believe that it is possible for training to make a difference in the performance of the people being trained. If we employ a professional with background and experience in our general area of operation, but unfamiliar with our specific activities, the obvious answer to that problem is training . . . or is it? It may be obvious to those who have spent much time in the training field, but it may be much less obvious to managers who have never had training as an immediate responsibility. In the technical world, there are always managers who like to think of themselves as "self-made," meaning that they got where they are without being trained, so they feel everyone else should go the same route. The organization has to believe that the most efficient and effective way to bring most employees up to production standard is with good training. If there is lack of organizational support, at any level, the training effort is certainly in jeopardy.

The *people doing the training* also need to be convinced that the specific training that's being offered, for specific deficiencies, will alleviate the specific problems. If not, there will be some things done incorrectly and some things not done that will cause the training to fail. For example, what most often happens in these situations is that insufficient time is allowed for preparation. This means that instructors aren't properly trained in how to train, the class material is inadequate, the audio or visual aids are poor or nonexistent, and the design itself may be hastily—thus improperly—done. This leads the instructors to feel uncomfortable with the proposed training effort, and they go into the training sessions with low enthusiasm. Worse, they may develop a kind of apathy toward the whole program. All of this ends up in poor training, and the lack of enthusiasm and the apathy quickly get transmitted to the trainees. It's a downward spiral that is difficult to escape!

The *people being trained* must also believe in the training. The technical and professional employees who come to the training sessions must accept and believe almost totally that the training they're about to engage in will result in overcoming some of the problems they see before them day to day on the job. Otherwise the training will go for naught. No matter how much support there is for the training on the part of the organization, no matter how well prepared the instructors are, and no matter how good the design and development of the course has been, the course will fail if the people being trained believe that the procedures, policies, or concepts being taught are wrong or useless.

Training *does* work! Most things in the world function properly or improperly in relation to how well or how poorly the people involved have been trained. So it has to be *good* training. It has to be designed well, implemented well, and utilized well. The students/employees getting the training have to be interested, involved, and desirous of learning what is provided. As we've seen, the information, thoughts, and skills being taught need to be pertinent to the jobs being performed. There has to be a close relationship between the training being done, the job being performed, and the trainees attending the instruction. The entire high-tech field is noted—more than anything else—for its rapid change and obsolescence. For that reason, we don't have time to train on "nice-to-know" subjects; we've got our hands full training in the essentials that are so vital to doing even the basic job! (For more details on evaluating training see Broadwell, 1976, pp. 182–191.)

DEVELOPING A TRAINING POLICY

Question: What is a training policy, and who should set it?

Answer: By policy we mean those rules, regulations, philosophies, and procedures that govern the activities of the organization at all levels of any organization.

These are things that are recognized as affecting the outcomes and results of the organization's activities. There are policies on things like tardiness and absenteeism and drug usage. The personnel department is always anxious to see that everyone knows and follows the policies with a high degree of consistency. There are policies on the use of money and how much money can be approved at what level in the organization. The accounting department is expected to keep close check on any abuse of these policies, in *all* departments, not just in the accounting department. The point is that there are organization-wide policies on many facets of the business, and everyone is expected to adhere to the policies or they are *violating organization policy.* In many organizations there are no uniform training policies. One group or section or department can have little interest in training, making no effort to get the new employees trained or oriented. Another part of the organization may be very excited and diligent about training, seeing that everyone gets all the training they need. This lack of uniformity is due to the failure of the organization—not the training department—to decide on a organization wide training policy. Most of the training done in many organizations is done because the people at the top of that particular part of the organization "believe" in training. If there were policies concerning training, they were uniform in nature, and people were held accountable for keeping policy, there would be more consistency in the training activities. There should be some very specific organizational policies on such things as:

Amount of Training

There should be a formal policy as to how much training people should get in given jobs or given time periods or at certain levels. It has simplified the training responsibilities of organizations when there is an overall policy on just how many days or hours of training certain people are supposed to have. If new engineers are to be trained, the amount and the nature of that training should be spelled out, so that some won't get it while others do. If people are to be trained as they attain a certain level, the amount of training should be clear, so that all people reaching that level will get the same amount and the same training courses.

Timing of Training

Not only is there a need for a uniform policy on how much training a person should get, but also one stating *when* that training should take place. It very discouraging to a new supervisor to see others get training, then have this new one go for years without any training at all. A supervisor who moves to the job with no training, then waits for three years to get formal training designed for "new supervisors," isn't going to profit much from the training. It now becomes a matter of "unlearning" a bunch of bad habits, learned before the training came along. Ideally, the policy should specify the limitations on how soon the training is given, and the upper limits on how long the person can go without training. For example, "All new support people should have four hours of computer orientation within the first six weeks of taking the job, but not before one week of work experience."

Priority of Trainees

It is an obvious fact of life that not everybody who needs training will get it, nor will the ones who get it receive it when they need it. That doesn't preclude honest effort on our part to do our best to try to make these things work out for the best of the employees. In fact, since not everyone can be selected for the training, there needs to be a policy stating—in a clear-cut fashion—which people get first call on the training being offered. The policy should be a broad one that not only designates who will get trained first, but also how this decision will be made. Arrangements should be made for periodic "needs analyses" to be made to determine who needs what training and when. The decision usually is made on the basis of where the long-range payoff is the greatest as a result of the training. Typically, this isn't where the *most* training is, but where the results are greatest to the organization. It may be that training a few technical people in a new use of a sophisticated new process will have a much greater impact on profits or research or savings than some other kind of mass training. The training of the few may tend to "smooth out" the operation and get rid of a few headaches, but not do a great deal for the overall direction of the organization. The formula for such a policy decision is to subtract the cost of training from the cost of the deficiency (what the poor performance is costing the organization) and see how much payoff there is. If the difference isn't great enough, there can be a decision to forego the training. At least the decision will be on the basis of a recognized policy, not the whim of a supervisor who "made it on my own without training."

Selection Process

A specific policy should exist that spells out who has the responsibility for selecting the trainees and the selection criteria. Supervisors should not be allowed to use training as some kind of reward, since the people going to training activities should be selected on the basis of need, not reward. By spelling out who has the job of selecting the trainees, there is a measure of accountability for the selection process. This will help the uniformity in student selection. It will also help supervisors know when they are doing their job properly, since the training policy will give measurement criteria for appraisals. If supervisors are evaluated on their following policy, they will have reason for following the policies! Those supervisors who do not provide for the training will be in violation of the training policy, hence not considered as doing a satisfactory job.

A final word about having a policy. In many organizations there are policies, but too often they are put out by the training departments and don't represent the thinking or conviction of all departments that will be taking advantage of the training offered. Good supervisors actually urge the organization to develop a specific training policy so they will have some guidelines, rather than just leaving such an important thing up to some nebulous decision-making process as whim or feelings. Training is an important part of the employees' career development. It is important to the successful completion of the job. It will determine, many times, just how successful the organization will be in handling the day-to-day job, the meeting of long-range goals, and staying up with the competition. There is ample evidence that technical and professional people will be more likely to stay with an organization that allows them opportunities to keep abreast of their fields and to explore others. For the most part, technical and professional people are used to a learning environment. For all these reasons, they should be in an environment where there is a training policy that clearly states what training they will be offered, how much, and when the training will be available to them. The environment should also include supervisors who follow the policies!

TRAINING VERSUS DEVELOPMENT

Question: What is the difference between training and development?

Answer: There is no ready answer to this, and there are those who like to debate it for hours.

For the sake of dealing with it here, let's just say that, generally, "training" deals with the job itself, the immediate task to be performed, whereas "development" refers to the long-range usage of potential. Some like to point out that training is most often the result of performance appraisals, where we look at people in specific jobs, find their their weaknesses, and provide training to overcome those shortcomings. At best, we would look into the future no further than the next job, as far as training is concerned. We might send someone to a training program so that they would be prepared to take on the next assignment—which is usually similar to the one they now have.

Development would come from looking at some kind of potential assessment, determining where there were areas that could be developed for future activities in the organization—perhaps quite different from the present job. Development is more closely tied to "career," then, than is training. We look at people and ask ourselves, and perhaps them, too, "Where would this person fit into the organization five years from now?" While some of this is "crystal-ball gazing," it also comes from good observation and interviewing powers on the part of the supervisor. With a little practice, we can begin to recognize where employees get "turned on" by certain assignments and get "turned off" by others. We can also see eyes light up at prospects of certain kinds of jobs and eyes go dim at the mention of other kinds of jobs. This doesn't mean that a person is always going to be good at what they like to do. That's where assessing gets to be more scientific. We give the employee certain jobs to do that are different from what they are now doing, let them have some training, then see how well they do in the *skills* of the job, not just the *interest* in the work being done. Good supervisors have profiles of their employees, including lists of things the employee is good and bad at in the present job, and some prediction of future strengths and weaknesses in other potential jobs.

PERSONAL DEVELOPMENT

Question: Are there some things that technical and professional people can do, on their own, that will help them develop?

Answer: It is perhaps one of the most unique characteristics of professional people that they do such a good job of staying current with the state of the art of their professions, and have an eagerness about developing themselves.

It usually goes without saying that most technical and professional people thrive on technical and professional information about their own fields. Even so, with all this desire to learn as much as possible about what's going on in their related world, there are still some things they can and should do to better themselves for their own well-being and their careers. Let's look at some of them.

Goal Setting

While most technical and professional people keep current in their professions, many of them do not have very specific goals in their lives in general. Most of them set short-range goals which got met with the finishing of their education and getting of a job. Many get restless in the jobs they have, many times because they don't get the satisfaction they had hoped to have in the work world. Much of this is due to the absence of even short-range goals and, most assuredly, the lack of long-range direction. For their lives to become more meaningful, the successful ones seem to come to grips with just where it is they're trying to go in life. Some do it more formally than others, and some hesitate even to think about "life," as though it were somehow a nontechnical thing to think about. Some think of such activity as being almost nonprofessional. It isn't, of course, and most of us are better off when we take the time to ask simple questions, such as "Where would I like to be five years from now?" or "If I were really doing what I would like to be doing the rest of my life, what would I be doing?"

Reading

It's not too difficult to get highly technical people to read a journal in their field, or most any kind of technical publication. This is certainly commendable and is almost an essential activity for staying useful in a chosen profession. The accelerating technological obsolescence that we've talked about before virtually demands this kind of diligence. But this isn't the end of developing. There is more to developing one's self than just reading technical journals. This is a limiting thing, suggesting that "that's all there is to my life." The well-rounded person is one who knows more about the world than just the everyday technical things with which he or she works. Good development means reading things of broader interest, even good fiction—escapism isn't a bad thing for those who spend so much time concentrating on logic and reason and technical things—and books on supervision or managing people, as well as managing the job. Good, healthy respect for good writing will expand the mind as quickly as anything we can do. It's one of the best ways to expand the mind in a controlled way.

Attending Meetings

Just as there needs to be development along reading lines, attending meetings, conferences, and seminars will do much to offer a broadening experience. We need to be somewhat selective, of course, since not all sessions are that good for us. (There is often some expense involved that can be considerable if we have traveling and lodging to pay.) We look at these meetings as growth opportunities, not just chances to travel or get out of the office. If we go to a regional or national meeting, we should give careful consideration ahead of time to all the possible sessions we can attend, done by studying the brochure and advanced announcements, as well as the usual registration packets that come out. This way we don't have to make quick, un-thought-out decisions on the spur of the moment. There is another legitimate activity that we can engage in at these conferences besides going to the meetings. A major benefit of such activities is associating with people from other organizations, doing similar or even quite different things from those we are doing. This kind of sharing is most beneficial to our staying fresh. Otherwise we tend to become rather inbred in our thinking and our knowledge. This association will often trigger our thought processes into action where they've been slowed down by the routine of our routine job.

Personal Effort

Much of what we've said about self-development has really been taking advantage of what others have done for us: provided books or journal subscriptions; paid our way to conferences; provided us with appraisals or assessments of ourselves. Now it's time for us to do some things on our own. We make a commitment to ourselves to become a better engineer or professional or technical research person; but we also make a commitment to become a generally better all-round individual. We take some long looks at ourselves to see what we are and what we'd like to be. We decide on some goals —short and long. We decide that we don't like certain things about ourselves, but at the same time liking ourselves well enough to decide we're worth saving! So we go to work on the deficiencies. We improve our writing skills or our speaking skills with practice and by signing up for courses at night, if necessary. We decide we aren't broad enough in our knowledge of literature, so we read some of the classics. We decide we have certain quirks in our personality that irritate people, and we figure out how to do better—then practice, practice, and practice changing those things. We look at our ability to utilize our time, then work at better time managing. We decide that we're getting too ingrown and stale by working too long each day, and not taking breaks and not leaving the desk for lunch, so we take the breaks, go out for lunch, and take our holidays and vacations by going somewhere and doing something—besides thinking about the job. We use hobbies as a means to escape the routine of the job and as a way to keep our minds renewed from time to time. All of these things have their place but are often foreign to the technical and professional people. And most important of all: we need a private life of some kind. We need time with the family and a chance to do something with them that we'll remember for a long time to come. We need to stop every once in awhile and just smell the roses. It's pretty nice if those roses are some we've grown in our own garden in our own dedicated spare time!

CONCLUSION

Training is not a luxury that some can afford, or something we do if there is time and nothing else is more pressing. Training and developing people is an essential part of the operation of any business. The extent to which people are trained and trained well, on the right subjects and skills, at the right time, is the extent to which an operation will function properly for any time at all. We train people so that they will be able to do their jobs more effectively. In a seemingly selfish way, the organization probably benefits first and most from well-trained people. In the long run, it is a mutually beneficial activity. Development of employees for future tasks and to take advantage of their potential makes development a strong key to the future well-being of an organization. There are many reasons why we should believe in training and developing people, and many reasons why we should have an organizational policy and philosophy that supports training and has specified who, when, and what about training. But while there are a number of economic and motivational reasons for training, there are very few, if any, justifiable reasons why we should ignore the training and development of any employees who we expect to perform but who cannot because they don't know what they're trying to do. The benefits are so numerous that more and more supervisors and organizations are realizing that there is no substitute for adequate training. It is, in fact, a profit-making, money-saving part of the operation in itself!

References

Albrecht, Karl. (1979). *Stress and the manager.* Englewood Cliffs, NJ: Prentice-Hall.

Barnard, C. I. (1938). *The functions of the executive.* Cambridge, MA: Harvard University Press.

Barnes, W. (1972, July). Linear responsibility charting. *Industrial Engineering,* pp. 17–19.

Benson, Herbert. (1975). *The relaxation response.* New York: William Morrow.

Bower, Sharon A., & Bower, Gordon H. (1976). *Asserting yourself.* Reading, MA: Addison-Wesley.

Broadwell, Martin M. (1976). *The supervisor as an instructor.* Reading, MA: Addison-Wesley.

Carkhuff, R. R. (1972). *The art of helping.* Amherst, MA: Human Resource Development Press.

Cummings, T. G., Molloy, Edmond S., & Glen, Roy H. (1975). Intervention strategies for improving productivity and the quality of working life. *Organizational Dynamics, 4*(1), 52–68.

Ellis, A., & Harper, R. (1975). *A new guide to rational living.* North Hollywood, CA: Wilshire.

Faber, Nancy. (1984). Computer widows bring their marriages back to life with input from counselor Jean Hollands. *People, 12*(3), 93–94.

Holmes, Thomas H., & Rahe, Richard H. (1967). The social readjustment scale. *Journal of Psychosomatic Research.* (11) 212–218.

Kübler-Ross, Elizabeth. (1969). *On death and dying.* New York: Macmillan.

Kushner, Harold. 1981. *When bad things happen to good people.* New York: Avon.

Laird, Dugan, & House, Ruth. (1984). *Interactive classroom instruction.* Glenview, IL: Scott, Foresman.

McCall, Morgan W., Jr. and Lombardo, Michael M. (1983). What makes a top executive. *Psychology Today, 17*(2), 26–31.

McFarlan, T. Warren. (1981). Portfolio approach to information systems. *Harvard Business Review, 59*(5), 142–150.

Massey, Morris. (1978). *What you are isn't necessarily what you will be* [Videotape]. Farmington Hills, MI: CBS-Fox Video.

Parsons, H. M. (1974, March). What happened at Hawthorne? *Science, 183*, 922–931.

Pritikin, Nathan, with Patrick M. McGrady, Jr. (1979). *The Pritikin program for diet and exercise.* New York: Grosset and Dunlap.

Renwick, Patricia A., & Lawler, Edward E. (1978). What you really want from your job. *Psychology Today, 11*(12), 53–58, 60, 62, 65, 118.

Robertson, Laurel, Flinders, Carol, & Godfrey, Bronwen. (1976). *Laurel's kitchen.* Petaluma, CA: Nilgiri Press.

Shakespeare, William. (1953). *23 plays and the sonnets,* Thomas Marc Parrott, Edward Hubler, & Robert Stockdale (Eds.), New York: Scribner's.

Smith, Lendon. (1981). *Foods for healthy kids.* New York: McGraw-Hill.

Synders, Jan, & Lasden, Martin. (1980). Managing programmers to work harder and happier. *Computer Decisions, 12*(10), 34–35, 39–42.

Thompson, P. H., & Dalton, G. W. (1970, January). Performance appraisal: managers beware. *Harvard Business Review,* pp. 149–157.

University Associates. (1976). Role functions in a group. In J. William Pfeiffer and John E. Jones (Eds.), *The annual handbook for group facilitators* (pp. 136–138). La Jolla, CA: University Associates.

Winship, Barbara, & Kelley, Jan. (1976). A verbal response model of assertiveness. *Journal of Counseling Psychology, 23,* 215–220.

Appendix

TIPS FROM CHAPTER ONE

General Guidelines

To respond to the characteristics of technical and professional people, technical managers can:

1. Keep the big picture in focus for their employees
2. Let their own behavior be an example of good interpersonal relations
3. Groom the people they supervise for professional growth and advancement
4. Absorb hostility
5. Contain the cost of conflict
6. Allow considerable technical freedom within agreed-upon limits
7. Demonstrate respect for personal values
8. Manage the flow of information between their groups and the rest of the organization
9. Manage the flow of information within their groups

TIPS FROM CHAPTER TWO

Managing People in General

Like managers of people in general, technical managers should:

1. Know employees as individuals
2. Manage them as individuals
3. Spot changes for the better that deserve reinforcement
4. Identify concerns that call for exploration or reassurance
5. Manage the job environment to control turnover
6. Manage the job itself to control performance

TIPS FROM CHAPTER THREE

Attitudes for Successful Communication with Nontechnical People

To communicate successfully with nontechnical people, technical managers should understand that:

1. Nontechnical is not nonintelligent
2. Nontechnical people are equal contributors in organizational success
3. Complete accuracy in word usage is not a requirement for nontechnical understanding
4. Technical people need to develop nontechnical vocabularies

Hints for Successful Communication with Nontechnical People

To communicate successfully, technical managers should always:

1. Give instructions in nontechnical terms, as much as possible
2. Avoid complicated explanations; *more* technical words don't increase nontechnical information
3. Get feedback to check understanding
4. Work at understanding why people act and react as they do

TIPS FROM CHAPTER FOUR

Combatting Stereotypes of Technical People

To fight stereotypes about technical and professional people, technical managers can:

1. View the stereotypes as the "working hypotheses" others have about their group, and set out to change these stereotypes without taking them personally
2. Accumulate "points" for their group by taking part in high-visibility activities with their own supervisors and peers
3. Respond rationally to criticism
4. Know the "unwritten rules" and tell their people about them so the staff won't be caught off guard
5. Openly discuss the reality of dependence in the organization and the need for independence in their group
6. Avoid "battles to the death"

Combatting Stereotypes about Management

To combat unfair stereotypes of management, technical managers can:

1. Distinguish between a strong career orientation and ruthlessness
2. Identify the conditions of conflict with management
3. Demonstrate the steady, systematic behavior that gives them credibility with their employees just as it does with higher management

Handling Shifts in Priorities

To handle shifts in priorities, technical managers should:

1. Simply steel themselves for embarrassment
2. Tell other people involved as soon as possible and as straightforwardly as possible
3. Treat the disappointment of other people involved as they would any other important loss
4. Analyze the impact of the change and help make the needed adjustments

TIPS FROM CHAPTER FIVE

Containing the Organizational Costs of Stress

To contain the organizational costs of stress, technical managers can:

1. Allow themselves—and others—some emotional distance
2. Recognize that what they can observe and manage is *behavior,* not motives or attitudes
3. Have a clear mental picture of how things would look if they looked "just right"
4. Plan a systematic course of action to cut their losses when necessary
5. Avoid waving "red flags"
6. Present ideas assertively but not aggressively

Containing the Personal Costs of Stress

To contain the personal costs of stress, technical managers can:

1. Use deep-breathing exercises and muscle relaxation exercises at intervals during a high-stress day to help reduce the physical and emotional wear and tear
2. Practice deep-breathing and muscle relaxation exercises at home *regularly*
3. Participate regularly in an aerobic exercise such as biking or swimming
4. Get ample sleep
5. Eat nutritiously and moderately
6. Give themselves verbal mental encouragement

TIPS FROM CHAPTER SIX

Flexible Management

Technical managers can build team cooperation by following the guidelines for *flexible* (not *formula*) management:

1. Notice how each employee works best: when each works best on a task with close direction; when each works best with little direction on the task, but with support in coordinating teamwork
2. Distinguish between tasks that require close direction and those that do not
3. Identify organizational conditions that require close direction and those that do not
4. Be familiar with several interaction models that can be adapted to suit their own personalities and a given situation

TIPS FROM CHAPTER SEVEN

Building Team Cooperation

To foster team effort, technical managers can systematically try to:

1. Know employees individually
2. Complement group skills
3. Provide feedback
4. Reward group effort

Preventing Polarization

To prevent polarization, technical managers can:

1. Name the problem and encourage people to talk about it
2. Give employees feedback about the effects of the problem on the group's work
3. Get employees' help to remove blocks to group effort and to try new patterns of behavior

TIPS FROM CHAPTER EIGHT

Providing Long-Term Motivation

The following don't provide long-term motivation:

1. More money
2. Improved working conditions

Providing Long-Term Motivation

The following provide long-term motivation:

1. Achievement
2. Recognition/status
3. Meaningful work assignments
4. Meeting personal needs
   a. Belonging to a group
   b. Feeling important

TIPS FROM CHAPTER NINE

General Guidelines to Delegation

To delegate successfully, technical managers should:

1. Delegate to the lowest level of competency in the organization
2. Get the job done through others
3. Use flexible delegation styles

Reasons for Delegation

Technical managers should delegate so as to:

1. Motivate people
2. Develop people
3. Build teamwork
4. Provide supervisory time for other functions
5. Assess employee potential
6. Give a sense of achievement

TIPS FROM CHAPTER TEN

Removing Obstacles to Good Performance

To remove obstacles to good performance, technical managers should:

1. Set good job standards, approved by the organization
2. Identify acceptable, personal standards of the supervisor
3. Orient standards to the *job,* not to other employees
4. Communicate standards ahead of performance time
5. Train employees to standard, as needed
6. Give employees feedback on their performance—while they are performing

Interviewing the Poor Performer

To interview the poor performer, technical managers should take the following steps:

1. Have the documentation in order
2. Pick a time and place conducive to an uninterrupted interview
3. Put the employee at ease
4. Establish the purpose of the interview
5. Establish ground rules and procedures for conducting the interview and the follow-up
6. Allow the employee to remove "demerits" in the follow-up

Taking Disciplinary Action

When taking disciplinary action, technical managers should:

1. Use discipline as a management tool
2. Take corrective action quickly while the activity is going on
3. Use documentation skillfully

Keeping Management Informed

To keep management informed, technical managers should:

1. Avoid giving management too many details
2. Inform to prevent surprises
3. Let management help in setting standards for less tangible work areas
4. Use management's help on raises, promotions, and discharges
5. Stick by their decisions but learn from them

TIPS FROM CHAPTER ELEVEN

Getting Technical Updates

To effectively get/give technical updates, technical managers should:

1. Know where to find the key people for a given project
2. Sift through data for information
3. Spell out who relates to whom and how

TIPS FROM CHAPTER TWELVE

Preparing for a Technical Presentation

To prepare for a technical presentation, technical managers should:

1. Know the topic
2. Know the audience
3. Know themselves

Know Your Topic

Knowing your topic means to:

1. Know the subject well enough to outline it
2. Consider questions the audience might ask and be prepared with information
3. Decide on certain areas of the topic in which you just don't have expertise
4. Determine what these people need to take away with them

Suggestions for an Effective Presentation

During the presentation, you should:

1. Look and act confident
2. Use good body language
3. Deliver a solid opening and closing

TIPS FROM CHAPTER THIRTEEN

Reasons for Holding a Meeting

Following are good reasons for conducting meetings:

1. To inform or report
2. To persuade or sell
3. To organize or reconstruct
4. To get information or ideas
5. To brainstorm or solve problems
6. To meet some requirements

Preparing for a Successful Meeting

To prepare for a successful meeting, technical managers should:

1. Determine the purpose of the meeting
2. Prepare themselves (mentally and physically)
3. Build an agenda
4. Prepare the participants
   a. Notify people ahead of time
   b. Assign roles
5. Prepare the place

Conducting a Successful Meeting

To conduct a successful meeting, technical managers should:

1. Begin in a positive, businesslike manner
2. Use the participants
3. Watch for hidden agendas
4. Prepare a strong close
5. Follow up

TIPS FROM CHAPTER FOURTEEN

Negotiating Principles

To negotiate successfully, technical managers should:

1. Know what to keep and what to give up
2. Know the other person
3. Understand the situation they're going into, facts, figures, and so on
4. Use the personalities involved in a positive way
5. Get some kind of agreement as soon as possible

TIPS FROM CHAPTER FIFTEEN

Cushioning Stress Resulting from Changes

To cushion the stress that results from changes in the work situation, technical managers can:

1. Expect it and treat it as a "natural" sequence of event
2. Listen to employees blow off steam without reacting adversely

Handling a Reduction in Team Effort

To accept a temporary setback in team effort, technical managers can:

1. Expect it
2. Listen
3. Accommodate some overdependent behavior
4. Redirect behavior that is headed through improper channels

Helping Group Members Work through Grief

To help members of a group as they work through the stages of grief, technical managers can:

1. Expect employees to go through this sequence when they've experienced a loss: denial, anger, bargaining, depression, acceptance
2. Listen
3. Give employees reassurance of their worth without minimizing their loss
4. Avoid giving advice, telling "war stories," and asking a lot of direct questions

Absorbing Individual Reactions to Change

To absorb some of the dissonance as individual reactions to the change unfold at different rates, technical managers can:

1. Expect different reaction rates from different employees
2. Listen

Index